Introduction...

d since
e of my
e of work,
cisive way,
ritish?
or us and
me.

anagers it
ter time to
ompany.
he venues,
years to

bringing
e a Pilot
own the
he issues
d all
re able to
wing our
3s.

nging rapidly
y for a group
a piece of
vity which
e no other.
n and that
the world we

Artistic Director

Let us know what you think

see your comments posted

(normal text charge applies

81471038 and

D1421531

Roy Williams

Roy Williams turned to writing full time in 1990. He graduated from Rose Bruford College in 1995 with a first class BA Hons degree in Writing and participated in the 1997 Carlton Television screenwriters' course. The **No Boys Cricket Club** won him nominations for the TAPS Writer of the Year Award 1996 and for New Writer of the Year Award 1996 by the Writers' Guild of Great Britain. He was the first recipient of the Alfred Fagon Award 1999 for **Starstruck**, which also won the 31st John Whiting Award and the EMMA Award 1999. His other plays include: **Night and Day**, **Josie's Boys**, **Souls**, **Local Boy**, **The Gift**, **Clubland** (winner of the Evening Standard Award for Most Promising Playwright), **Fallout** and **Sing Yer Heart Out for the Lads**. Screenplays include **Bedrens** and **Offside** and his radio plays include **Tell Tale**, **Westway** and **Homeboys**, which was broadcast as part of the Radio 4 First Bite Young Writers' Festival. He also wrote **Babyfather** for BBC TV.

Roy Williams is currently working on a commission for the RSC, **Days of Significance** (Swan Theatre, Stratford Upon Avon) and a play with musician Damon Albarn for the National Theatre.

Interview with Roy Williams

What was the inspiration for Sing Yer Heart Out for the Lads?
I wanted to write a bigger play, something that would challenge me as a writer. I was interested in themes that I had touched on before, about racism and cultural identity, but I wanted to write something that would be closer to the bone.

I'm mad about football and one day I was sitting in a pub in Birmingham. It was a nice pub and we were watching the England – Germany game, it was Euro 2000 and we won, one – nil (Shearer's goal). A group of young white men came into the pub to watch the match and the atmosphere became really uncomfortable. They were loud and raucous, chanting anti-German, xenophobic stuff and then having a go at Beckham. The things they said about Posh (Victoria Beckham) were obscene, you'll recognise some of it in Barry's speech and I've edited the worst bits out. There was one other black person in the pub and we made eye contact, I think we were both thinking the same thing: any minute now there is going to be a comment about a black player and then all this racism will come pouring out. I thought about it on the way home and realised that I had my story.

The National Theatre had commissioned me to write something and so I pitched this idea to them. I made the decision to base the play on the next England – Germany match that was coming up. Of course, as a football fan, I was gutted that we lost, but I was happy as a playwright, because it made a much better story.

Are the characters in the play based on real people?
The characters in the play are a hybrid of people who were in the pub that day in Birmingham and people on the estate where I grew up. I had friends at school whose houses I'd go to for tea. I'd meet their parents and they'd have these racist views. I'm not trying to knock these people down but I'm trying to be truthful. Race is revealed in different ways and all the characters have different levels of racist opinion. Alan is the bigot with a briefcase but Lawrie's racism is brutal and instinctive. To explore where it comes from, you have to get it out in the open and not be apologetic. I feel that whenever racism is brought up on television or in film, it's quite cowardly, one of the few films that get it right is Spike Lee's **Do The Right Thing** – it erupts and makes it scary. I have to present people that I don't agree with, because they exist.

All the men in the play seem to have missing fathers, is this a deliberate theme?
It is a common thread in my work, perhaps because my own father was absent, but it wasn't a deliberate decision, it's just the way it came about. Lawrie, for example, is still working out what it is to be a man, his transition to adulthood is still going on and Alan is well placed to exploit his vulnerability.

What were the highs and lows of writing the play?
The fun part of writing this play was setting it in a pub that's full of people, it's the largest cast I've ever written, the size of a football team! My favourite bit of the play is when they are talking about the different football strips.

But it was a weird thing to write, having to look up all these far right websites. It made me realise how people can lose any sense of morality in order to try to belong. One of the reviewers of the original production said the line that summed it all up for her was the last line, "don't lose yourself." While everyone is trying to stake their claim to being British, they don't see what they are doing to each other, and themselves, in that process. Barry is trying so hard, when he's talking about football or about Posh, but it's all about trying to belong. For me, the soul of the play is about what it means to be British, and how you define that.

What advice would you give to young writers?
Just go for it. Write it down and don't talk about it too much or you'll never get it written. Make sure you've got something to say and that you know what you're writing about.

Interview by Helen Cadbury June 2006

Sing Yer Heart Out for the Lads

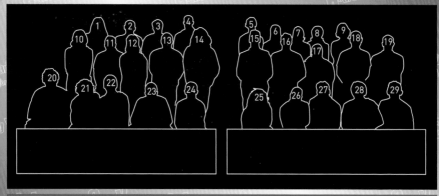

1. S. Seddon
2. M. Noddings
3. N. Hutton
4. P. Bankolé
5. C. Mnene
6. S. McLean
7. V. Biles
8. S. Orrock
9. E. Roberts
10. A. Smith
11. D. Bates
12. R. Chapman
13. C. Close
14. B. Cruse
15. D. Walmsley
16. T. Treloar
17. R. Williams
18. M. Romer
19. M. Monero
20. A. Falvey
21. S. Farnell
22. C. Gomez
23. D. Hart
24. T. Sawyer
25. R. Rowlinson
26. D. Youngman
27. M. Beasley
28. D. Cruden
29. M. North

Name:
Peter Bankolé
Position:
Barry

Career highlights

Training:
Rose Bruford College.

Theatre:
A Midsummer Night's Dream, As You Like It, The American Pilot, Venus and Adonis, Season of Migration to the North (RSC).

TV and film:
Casualty, Doctors, The Rotters' Club, The Bill, Dead to the World and Beefin' It.

Name:
Claude Close
Position:
Jimmy

Career highlights

Training: Manchester Polytechnic School of Theatre. **Theatre:** Neville's Island (Stephen Joseph Theatre), The Marriage Of Figaro (The New Vic), When We Are Married (Leicester Haymarket), Sweeney Todd (Oldham and Cheltenham), Crazy People (Manchester Library Theatre). **TV and film:** All Creatures Great and Small, Brookside, Heartbeat, Poirot, Hillsborough, Dalziel and Pascoe, Cold Feet, At Home with the Braithwaites, Coronation Street, and Max and Paddy.

Name:
Andrew Falvey
Position:
Lee

Career highlights

Theatre: Robin – Prince of Sherwood (Piccadilly Theatre), Spring Awakening (RSC), Forty Years On (UK Tour), A Midsummer Night's Dream (Cannizaro Park), A/S/L?, Bloodtide and Lord of the Flies (Pilot Theatre).**TV and film:** Johnny and the Dead, The Famous Five, The Frighteners, Casualty, Watership Down, Doctors, Silent Witness, Northern Lights, The Bill. **Radio:** Under One Roof, Killer Country and Starting Out (BBC Radio 4), Westway.

Name:
Chad Gomez
Position:
Becks

Career highlights

Training: Anna Scher Theatre School and Rose Bruford College.

Theatre: Beautiful Thing (Pilot Theatre), American Blues (Greenwich Playhouse) and Romeo & Juliet (Bedlam Theatre). Aladdin and Dick Whittington (Broadway Theatre, Barking) and Dick Whittington (Wilde Theatre, Bracknell).

TV and film: EastEnders and the BBC TV film Summer in the Suburbs.

Name:
Darren Hart
Position:
Duane

Career highlights
Theatre:
Henry IV parts 1 & 2, His Dark Materials (Royal National Theatre),
The Stones, Wam Bam (NT Education), Breathing (Latchmere), Bintou (Arcola), Da Boyz, Shoot to Win, 20,000 Leagues Under the Sea (Theatre Royal Stratford East).

TV and film:
Holby City.

Radio:
Silver Street.

Name:
Neville Hutton
Position:
Phil

Career highlights

Training: Rose Bruford College.
Theatre: The Play What I Wrote (Nick Brook Productions), Epsom Downs (Southampton Nuffield Theatre),The Elephant Man (Worcester Swan), Lord of the Flies (Pilot Theatre), The Marriage of Figaro, Up 'n' Under, The Government Inspector (Harrogate Theatre) Edward II, Privates on Parade (Leicester Haymarket).
TV and film: Hope and Glory (BBC), Casualty (BBC), Silent Witness (BBC) and Dream (Acier Productions).

Name:
Suzann McLean
Position:
Sharon & Assistant Director

Career highlights
Training: Italia Conti Academy Theatre: Measure for Measure (RNT), Romeo & Juliet (Theatre-By-The-Lake), I Have Before Me… Rwanda (National Tour) Vengeance (Hackney Empire), Blue Girl (Vienna's English Theatre), Angie Baby (Young Vic)**TV and film:** To Strike A Chord, Wishbaby, Casualty, Coupling II, Grange Hill, The A-Force, Little Miss Jocelyn (BBC) Jesus Christ Superstar.**Directing:** The Underworld (Peacock Theatre), Gospel Glory (Luton), Going Local (Stratford Circus), Songs of the Century (London Palladium).

Name:
Charles Mnene
Position:
Bad T

Career highlights

Theatre:
The Bolt Hole, 59 Cups (Birmingham Rep), The Miller's Tale, The Pardoner's Tale (Kingsway College).

TV and film:
Shoot the Messenger, Dream Team, The Bill, Holby City, Undercover, Ahead of the Class, Doctors and The Chosen One. Life in Lyrics, Bird's Eye View, Chromophobia and leads in both The Great Ecstasy of Robert Carmichael and The Train Game.

Name:
Mark Monero
Position:
Mark

Career highlights

Theatre:
The Country Wife (Watford Palace Theatre), Animal (Soho Theatre), A Taste of Honey (Liverpool Playhouse).

TV and film:
Skins (E4), Gimme Gimme Gimme (BBC), Judge John Deed (BBC), Trial and Retribution (BBC), Waking the Dead (BBC), Eastenders (BBC), Sid and Nancy (Zenith).

Name:
Mikey North
Position:
Glen

Career highlights

Theatre:
Bottle Universe (Bush Theatre), The National Youth Music Theatre, Whitby Pavillion, Statement Theatre.

TV and film: Waterloo Road, The Bill, Doctors, The Chase, Mark of Cain, A Mind of her Own, Pawn.

Radio: Baguettes and Barms (BBC Radio 4).

Name:
Sally Orrock
Position:
Gina

Career highlights
Training: Drama Studio London.
Theatre: Get Carter (Red Shift Theatre Co, National Tour & Edinburgh Festival 2006), The Minotaur (Sheffield Crucible), Macbeth, A Midsummer Night's Dream & Henry V (Nuffield Theatre, Southampton), Jacques & His Master (Young Vic Studio), A Midsummer Night's Dream (Queens Theatre, Hornchurch), Kvetch (Battersea Arts Centre), Educating Rita (European Tour, Tour de Force Theatre Co.), Hamlet (Horla Theatre Company).
TV and film: Couriers (Kalizma Films), Hearts from the Butcher (Clocktower Productions).
Voice-Overs: MTV, L'Oreal.

Name:
Tom Sawyer
Position:
Jason

Career highlights

Training: The Poor School.

Theatre: Venezuela (Arcola Theatre), Blowing Whistles (Jermyn Street Theatre), Someone's Son (Union Theatre).

TV and film: Family Affairs, Murder Prevention (Channel 5), The Murder Game (BBC), The Bill (Thames Talkback), Revolver (Diamond Bullets Prods/MTV).

Name:
Tim Treloar
Position:
Lawrie

Career highlights
Training: LAMDA.
Theatre: Henry V (National Theatre), The Beggar's Opera (Richmond Orange Tree), Rose Rage (Haymarket and tour) and Mountain Language (Royal Court). RSC: Thomas More, Believe What you Will, Sejanus, His Fall Back To Methuselah, Richard II, Romeo & Juliet.
TV and film: A Touch of Frost, Mine All Mine, Casualty, The Bill, Bombshell, The Brief, Foyle's War, Midsomer Murders, The Bench and Bomber. Wondrous Oblivion.
Radio: BBC Radio Rep.

Name:
Deka Walmsley
Position:
Alan

Career highlights
Theatre: Playing with Fire (National Theatre), Gaffer! (Southwark Playhouse/York Theatre Royal), Musik, Professor Bernhardi (Oxford Stage), Keepers of the Flame (RSC), Secret Heart, (Royal Exchange), Bones (Hampstead Theatre): Some Voices, Long Shadows (Live Theatre Co.) Mapping the Edge (Sheffield Crucible): Cooking with Elvis (Whitehall Theatre): Blood Brothers (West End) : Animal Farm (Northern Stage). **TV and film:** Dalziel and Pascoe, Rebus, 55 Degrees North, Dirty War, Waking the Dead, Doctors, Holby City, The Bill, Our Friends in the North.

Name:
Marcus Romer
Position:
Director/Artistic Director at Pilot Theatre

Career highlights

Training: Leeds University.
Directing: Lord of the Flies, Beautiful Thing, Road (Pilot Theatre) Abigail's Party and The Beauty Queen of Leenane (York Theatre Royal), The Twits (The Octagon, Bolton).
Adaptations: Rumblefish, Bloodtide.
Writing: Out of Their Heads, Taken Without Consent. Film and TV (acting): The Cops, Prime Suspect, Hillsborough, This is Personal, GBH, Emmerdale and Dalziel and Pascoe.

Name:
Emma Donovan
Position:
Designer

Career highlights

Training: Nottingham Polytechnic.
Productions: Abigail's Party and The Importance of Being Earnest (York Theatre Royal), Forward (Birmingham Rep), The Lion, The Witch and The Wardrobe, West Side Story, Plague of Innocence, Death of a Salesman, and The Wizard of Oz (Haymarket Theatre, Leicester).
Touring productions: Cut to the Chase (Tron Theatre), Eugene Onegin (Scottish Opera), Happy Natives (Soho Theatre), Beautiful Thing (Nottingham Playhouse).

Name:
James Farncombe
Position:
Lighting Designer

Career highlights

Productions: Lord of the Flies, Bloodtide (Pilot Theatre) Blonde Bombshells of 1943, Osama The Hero, (Hampstead Theatre, London), The Price, (Manchester Library Theatre), Blues For Mr Charlie (Tricycle), A View From The Bridge (The Octagon, Bolton) Three Sisters Birmingham Rep), Improbable Fiction (Stephen Joseph Theatre, Scarborough), To Kill A Mockingbird, West Side Story, (Leicester Haymarket Theatre), Beautiful Thing (Nottingham Playhouse), Abigail's Party (York Theatre Royal), Street Trilogy and Cloudburst (Theatre Absolute).

Name:
Sandy Nuttgens
Position:
Original Music & Sound Designer

Career highlights

Theatre: Bloodtide, Road and Rumblefish, Lord of the Flies (Pilot Theatre), A Clockwork Orange (Snap Theatre).

Film and TV: My Parents Are Aliens and Diana's Legacy (ITV), C4's Bare Knuckle Boxer, Who Killed Thomas Beckett?, Churchill's Girl and Agincourt (Channel 4), and The American West and Terry Jones Barbarians (BBC).

n ALL! collect them ALL! collect them ALL! collect them Al

Name:
Sweetie Irie
Position:
Songwriter

Career highlights

Collaborations: Aswad, Maxi Priest, Frankie Paul, Sanchez, Damon Albarn (Gorillaz), Roni Size, No Doubt, Gemma Fox, Kila Kela, Tubby T and Neneh Cherry.

Touring: Neneh Cherry.

Name:
Richard Ryan
Position:
Fight Director

Career highlights

Theatre and Opera: RSC, RNT, Royal Court, Royal Opera House, ENO, National Theatre of Ireland, Druid Theatre Company, York Theatre Royal, Sheffield Crucible, Colchester Mercury, Salisbury Playhouse, Birmingham Repertory Theatre, The Edinburgh International Festival, Cheek by Jowl and Pilot Theatre (Rumblefish, Beautiful Thing, Bloodtide, Road).

Film: Troy, The Last Legion and Stardust.

Sound Mixer	**Howie Taffs**
Audio Visual	**Boris Cruse**
Production Managers	**Mark Beasley and Matt Noddings**
Technical Stage Manager	**Stuart Farnell**
Company Stage Manager	**Dani Youngman**
Assistant Stage Manager	**Rachel Rowlinson**
Workshop leaders	**Bridget Foreman, Vicki Hackett, Sarah Osborne and Hannah Priddle**
Downloadable Education Pack	**Helen Cadbury**
Tour artwork	**www.stone-soup.co.uk**
Bobby (model)	**Paragon Creative Ltd www.paragoncreativeltd.co.uk**
Tour booking by	**makin projects. Tel: 01242 574 461 www.makinprojects.co.uk**

We would like to thank the following for their assistance with this production:

Fuller's Brewery
for their generous support

United Biscuits Ltd
for their generous donation of KP nuts

Carlsberg UK Carlsberg
for their generous support

Schweppes International Ltd
Gametime Leisure
Value Vend Limited
Minster Engraver
York Hospital
Gordon's Gin
York Brewery
Cameo Engraving Company
Ring-A-Till

pilot theatre

Pilot Theatre celebrates 25 years of creating, developing and touring pioneering and inspirational work.

Productions **Lord of the Flies** (winner of Manchester Evening News Award Best Touring Production), **East is East, Unsuitable Girls, Road, Bloodtide, Rumblefish, a/s/l?, Beautiful Thing** (winner of Manchester Evening News Award for Best Design and Most Promising Newcomer), **Mirad, Kiss of the Spiderwoman, TWOC, Out of their Heads, Abigail's Party, Walking the Tightrope, Beauty Queen of Leenane** and **Tale of Teeka**

Education Workshops, summer schools, post-show talks, school residencies, Youth Theatre, seminars and resource materials. Further information and booking – **education@pilot-theatre.com**

International British partner in Magic Net, a European Culture 2000 project connecting Companies across Europe in co-productions, artist exchanges, youth projects and conferences.

pilot-theatre.com Winner of 2003 and 2004 Audiences Yorkshire Award Best Use of Technology. Online chat room and discussion board, as well as video podcast downloads.

The Company
Artistic Director..................**Marcus Romer**
Administrative Producer.....**Mandy Smith**
Marketing Officer................**Elise Roberts**
Company Administrator......**Sarah Seddon**

Pilot Theatre would like to thank all the staff at York Theatre Royal

Pilot Theatre
York Theatre Royal
St. Leonard's Place
York
YO1 7HD
info@pilot-theatre.com

01904 635 755

pilot-theatre.com

"Pilot can be relied on to provide edgy, aggressive and innovative work"

The Guardian

The Twits
By Roald Dahl, adapted by David Wood
After a successful run at Octagon Theatre, Bolton at Christmas 05/06 Marcus Romer directs the show again at artsdepot, London, Christmas 06/07

Look Back in Anger
By John Osborne
Marcus Romer directs the angry young man, a co-production from Harrogate Theatre and Oldham Coliseum from February 2007

Looking for JJ – World Première
By Anne Cassidy, Adapted by Marcus Romer
Winner of the Booktrust Teenage Prize 2004, Shortlisted for the Whitbread Children's Book Award 2004 and the CILIP Carnegie Medal in 2005. A co-production with Unicorn Theatre, London and York Theatre Royal.
See www.lookingforjj.com

Catcher in their Eye – World Première
By Richard Hurford
The untold story of Mark Chapman's missing evening before he shot John Lennon

Bombshell – World Première
By Eva K. Mathijssen
An explosive new play by one of Holland's hottest writers seen through the eyes of a female suicide bomber

Leapers – World Première
By Mark Davies
Jumping off the page is a story of one lad and his mad obsession with Parkour and free running.

Be the first to know about all our work by joining our e-mail list at **pilot-theatre.com** or text club by texting the word PILOT to 07887 926101. All updates are free and your details will not be passed on to any third parties.

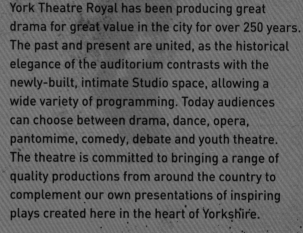

pilot theatre **inPARTNERSHIP** with **yorktheatre** royal

Hayfever

Pygmalion

Two

York Theatre Royal has been producing great drama for great value in the city for over 250 years. The past and present are united, as the historical elegance of the auditorium contrasts with the newly-built, intimate Studio space, allowing a wide variety of programming. Today audiences can choose between drama, dance, opera, pantomime, comedy, debate and youth theatre. The theatre is committed to bringing a range of quality productions from around the country to complement our own presentations of inspiring plays created here in the heart of Yorkshire.

Chief Executive	**Daniel Bates**
Artistic Director	**Damian Cruden**
General Manager	**Vicky Biles**
Production Manager	**Matt Noddings**
Director of Education	**Jill Adamson**
Head of Marketing	**Rachel Chapman**

Box Office 01904 623 568
www.yorktheatreroyal.co.uk

ARTS COUNCIL ENGLAND

CITY OF **YORK** COUNCIL

We have been working closely with Pilot for eight years; the partnership has grown over this time to become a permanent residency. The benefits this has brought to both companies are too many and various to list here, however some of the main advantages ought to be highlighted. Pilot's work is of great importance to the cultural development of young people. The company has a style that is unique and accessible to young people from early teens to late twenties, a notoriously difficult age group to engage in theatre. This has been achieved through a mixture of programming new and modern classics on the midscale and in the Studio. The work never feels as though it is imported from somewhere else, it never talks down and it is always challenging. The use of modern technology both on stage and on the internet is groundbreaking and has set the standard for many other companies to follow. The communication with young people is clear and uncompromising and the desire from schools and individuals to engage, unquestionable.

To have been a partner in the development of Pilot is something we at York Theatre Royal take great pride in. This partnership is heralded by the Arts Council as an example of good practice and both companies are often approached to share our methods with others both in the UK and abroad. For York Theatre Royal and our audience the benefits are great, we have been able to offer a far greater range of work for young people than we would ever have been able to on our own. Our staff have been able to develop new ways of partnership working, which can at times be difficult especially in a sector with limited resources and high demands.

We have made friendships that we would otherwise never have had, engaged with European companies, seen the name of York Theatre Royal travel the country, created exciting work, filled the theatre with young people, delivered workshops and summer schools and above all enriched the cultural life of York.

Damian Cruden
Artistic Director

tour dates

2006

York Theatre Royal
01904 623 568

23 Sep – 7 Oct
www.yorktheatreroyal.co.uk

Nottingham Playhouse
0115 941 9419

10 Oct – 14 Oct
www.nottinghamplayhouse.co.uk

Birmingham Repertory Theatre
0121 236 4455

18 Oct – 21 Oct
www.birmingham-rep.co.uk

New Wolsey, Ipswich
01473 295 900

7 Nov – 11 Nov
www.wolseytheatre.co.uk

artsdepot, London
0208 369 5454

14 Nov – 18 Nov
www.artsdepot.co.uk

2007

The Riverfront, Newport
01633 656757

1 Feb - 3 Feb
www.newport.gov.uk/riverfront

Contact Theatre, Manchester
0161 274 0600

6 Feb - 10 Feb
www.contact-theatre.org

Salisbury Playhouse
01722 320 333

13 Feb – 17 Feb
www.salisburyplayhouse.com

West Yorkshire Playhouse
0113 213 7700

20 Feb – 3 Mar
www.wyp.org.uk

Hackney Empire
0208 985 2424

22 Mar - 25 Mar
www.hackneyempire.co.uk

More dates in 2007 to be confirmed.
See pilot-theatre.com for details.

Roy Williams

Sing Yer Heart Out for the Lads

Methuen Drama

Published by Methuen Drama 2006

1 3 5 7 9 10 8 6 4 2

Methuen Drama
A & C Black Publishers Limited
38 Soho Square
London W1D 3HB
www.acblack.com

A CIP catalogue record for this book is available from the British Library

ISBN 10: 0 7136 8282 5
ISBN 13: 978 0 7136 8282 3

Typeset by Country Setting, Kingsdown, Kent
Printed and bound in Great Britain by
Bookmarque, Croydon, Surrey

Sing Yer Heart Out for the Lads

Characters

Jimmy, *white, mid fifties*
Alan, *white, late forties*
Lawrie, *white, mid thirties*
Phil, *white, mid thirties*
Gina, *white, early thirties*
Lee, *white, early thirties*
Mark, *black, early thirties*
Sharon, *black, early thirties*
Becks, *white, late twenties*
Barry, *black, early twenties*
Jason, *white, early twenties*
Duane, *black, early teens*
Glen, *white, early teens*
Bad T, *black, early teens*

Sing Yer Heart Out for the Lads was first performed at the
National Theatre, London, on 2 May 2002

Act One

*King George public house, south-west London. This section of the bar area is decorated with flags of St George. Windows, walls, tables etc. A huge TV screen is draped in the corner. **Jimmy** is assembling rows of stools and chairs in front of the TV screen. **Gina**, his daughter, is writing names on stickers with a felt-tip pen and sellotaping them on the stools, one by one.*

Gina   There had better not be any trouble.

Jimmy   Lee will be here.

Gina   Lee?

Jimmy   He'll sort 'em out.

Gina   Lee is juss as bad as they are.

Jimmy   He's a copper.

Gina   Yer point being?

Jimmy   He's a copper Gina, nuff said.

Gina   Get a few pints down him, you'll see. I should know.

She looks at her dad, who has the remote for the TV.

You awright over there, Dad?

Jimmy   Can't get this fuckin thing to work.

Gina   Well, I don't want to hear that, do I?

Jimmy (*looks at screen*) Fucking static.

Gina   Leave it to me. (*Takes the remote.*) Wat you done?

Jimmy   Nuttin, I was . . .

Gina   Pissin about.

Jimmy   Oi!

Gina *presses the button on the remote. The screen becomes all blue.*

Jimmy   Piece of shit.

Gina   You finish with the names, I'll do this.

Jimmy   You put Lawrie at the front?

Gina   Yeah. On second thoughts, stick him near the back. He'll only piss about. (*To TV*.) Come on, come on!

Jimmy   Ain't workin.

Gina   The satellite signal ain't comin through. Dad do me a favour, check that the cable for the dish is plugged in.

Jimmy   Have already.

Gina   What about the dish outside?

Jimmy   Done that.

Gina   Then what is its fucking problem? Where's the instruction manual?

Jimmy   Behind the bar.

Gina   Well, giss it.

Jimmy *hands over the manual.*

Gina   If I said it once, I've said it a hundred times.

Jimmy   Oh, don't start.

Gina   Becks is nuttin but a little thief. You should know better.

Jimmy   It was a steal.

Gina   Here we go. Come on baby, come on, come on! (*A picture comes on.*) Yes!

Jimmy   It'll be typical if they called the match off. It's pissing down. We ain't gonna win.

Gina   That's patriotic.

Jimmy   Kevin Keegan is a fucking muppet. Have you seen his line-up? (*Holds up paper.*) Tosser!

Gina   A bit of faith Dad.

Jimmy   Bollocks. He oughta fuck off back to Fulham, be Al Fayed's bleeding lapdog! Never mind manage the national team. A bit of faith, my arse!

Gina   What's wrong?

Jimmy   Southgate. Keegan has given him the midfield
holding position. The midfield holding position, I have trouble
even saying it. Look, Southgate is a defender, bloody good one,
no argument, but a good passer of the ball, he ain't! I mean
Keegan's got Dennis Wise in the frame, why didn't he pick
him? Use him? If that ain't torture for the lad, to be picked,
for the squad, but only to be left on the touchline, whilst some
muppet makes a right bollock of the position he's blinding at.
I ask you, where's the sense?

Gina   Southgate might surprise everyone.

Jimmy   Yeah, he'll be more shittier than I thought.

Gina   You won't be watchin the match then. You can clear
out the backyard at last.

Jimmy   Now, I didn't say I weren't gonna watch it. I'm juss
stating my opinion, thass all.

Gina   Who's up front?

Jimmy   Owen and Cole. Andy fucking Cole. Don't get me
started on him. Our last game at Wembley an' all. Fucking
Keegan.

Gina   Does Andy Gray's face look blue to you?

Jimmy   Yeah.

Gina   I can't work out anything on this.

Jimmy   Let one of the boys do it. Look at his poxy formation.

Gina   Dad!

Jimmy   3–5–2! Poxy, continental shit!

Gina   Let me guess, 4–4–2?

Jimmy   Too right, 4–4–2. It's the English way of playing, go
with summin the lads are comfortable with, fer crying out
loud. 3–5–2!

Gina   Dad, yer boring me, shut up. This screen is giving me a headache.

Jimmy   Leave it. There'll be here soon.

Gina   He had better behave himself.

Jimmy   Who?

Gina   Lawrie.

Loud rap music coming from upstairs.

I don't believe him. (*Shouts.*) Glen! Turn it down! Glen! I tell you, I have had it with that bloody kid, he don't answer me no more!

Jimmy   I don't suppose his arsehole of a dad has been to see him.

Gina   You taking the piss? Glen, I swear to fucking Christ!

Jimmy   Let me go.

Gina   What do you think I'm going to do?

Jimmy   I've seen the way you two have been at it lately.

Gina   Drag his arse down here.

Jimmy *goes upstairs to get* **Glen**. **Gina** *lights up a cigarette.* **Jimmy** *returns with* **Glen**, *fourteen and with an attitude.*

Glen   Yeah, wat?

Gina   You deaf?

Glen   No.

Gina   Bloody should be, shit you play.

Glen   Ain't shit.

Jimmy   I can't even understand half the things they're saying.

Glen   Ca you ain't wid it guy.

Gina   English Glen, we speak English in here.

Glen *sucks his teeth.*

Gina   Excuse me, what was that?

Jimmy   Just tell me what you get from it.

Glen   Loads.

Gina   Yeah, like learning to call a woman a bitch.

Jimmy   You want to listen to music, Glen, the Kinks, Pink Floyd, the Who!

Glen   Who?

Jimmy   You taking the mick?

Glen   Old man.

Jimmy   Oi!

Gina   He ain't bin rude, Dad, he ends every sentence on man. And you know why? Because he's been hanging round with them black kids from the estate, when I specifically told him not to.

Glen   I don't remember that.

Gina   Do not take the piss, Glen.

Glen   Dem boys are awright, Mum.

Gina   No they are not.

Jimmy   Yer mum's right, son, I've seen them, they'll get you in bother.

Gina   They have already. I had to go down his school again, him and his black mates were picking on sum little Asian kid.

Jimmy   What, him? You sure?

Gina   One more strike and he's out.

Glen   I weren't picking on him.

Gina   Not what the teacher said.

Jimmy *clips him on the head*

Glen   Oi! Move man!

Jimmy   Little kid thinks he's a hard man now, eh? Picking on sum little Asian kid.

Glen   Mum?

Gina   Mum what?

Glen   Tell him.

Gina   You won't always have yer black mates backing you up, you know; one day, those Asian kids are gonna fight back. Prince Naseem was a little Asian kid once, look at him now.

Jimmy   Come on, take yer granddad on, if you think yer hard enuff.

Glen   Will you move from me please?

Gina   All right, Dad.

Jimmy   I hardly touched him.

Gina   It's enuff.

Jimmy   Little girl.

Gina   No more trouble, you hearing me?

Glen (*sees the fag in the ashtray*)   Was that you? Thought you quit.

Gina   I am addressing my addiction.

Glen   See her, Grandad, she fuckin goes on about me . . .

Gina   Oi, oi, less of the fuckin! If I want to have a smoke, I will have a smoke, so shut yer noise. The best thing you can do with temptation, is give in to it – Oscar Wilde.

Glen   Who dat, yer new boyfriend?

Gina   I don't even want to think about what they are not teaching you at school, I really don't. This whole area is going nowhere.

Glen's *mobile phone rings.*

Glen   Who dis? Awright man, wass up? You joke! Is it! Nuh man, wat? Yeah, I'm up fer it dread.

Gina *takes the phone off him.*

Glen   Giss it.

Gina (*to phone*)   Hello, this is Glen's mother speaking.

Glen   Mum, no.

Gina   I am afraid he cannot come to the phone, as he is in an awful lot of trouble, and will not be coming out for the next, twenty-five years, feel free to call back then. (*Hangs up.*)

Glen   Yer chat is dry.

Jimmy   What was that he was saying?

Gina   'Nuh man!'

Jimmy   'Yeah, I'm up fer it dread!' (*Laughs.*)

Glen   You don't hang up on T like that.

Gina   Who?

Glen   T. Bad T.

Gina   Is that his name?

Glen   His street name.

Gina   Wass yer street name?

Glen   Ain't got one yet.

Gina   Ah! (*Pats his cheek.*)

Glen   I won't get it now, yer shamin me.

Jimmy   Yer little whiner.

Glen   I'm sorry.

Gina   Like you mean it!

Glen   SORRY!

Gina   Good.

She pops her head round the other bar.

Gina   Dad, go give Kelly a hand.

Jimmy   Where you going?

Gina   Cellars.

Jimmy   Oi, Glenny boy.

Glen   Glen!

Jimmy   Don't get arsey with me, you little shit. Put these names on these seats. Some of the boys have reserved seats for the game.

Glen   Awright if I have a drink?

Jimmy   Yeah, of course it is, don't be silly.

Glen *strolls to the bar.*

Jimmy   Get out of it! He only believed me. And don't even think about sneaking one away, cos I'll know.

Glen   Cool.

Jimmy *leaves.* **Glen** *pours himself a shot of whisky.* **Jimmy** *creeps up from behind, clips him round the ear and takes the glass from him.*

Jimmy   Moby. (*Exits.*)

Glen *does as he is told, and puts down the stickers.* **Mark** (*black, early thirties*) *comes in.*

Glen   Awright, man?

Mark   Yeah.

Glen   Wass up?

Mark   What?

Glen   Nuttin.

Mark   Where's yer mum?

Glen   Cellar. Who are you?

Mark   Mark.

Glen   Mark who?

Mark   Juss Mark.

Glen   Awright man, easy guy!

His phone rings again.

(*Answers.*) Who dis? Awright man. It was my mum, weren't it.
She took it off me, wat was I supposed to do, lick her down or
summin? Yeah, so wass up? Wat now? Yeah, well why didn't
you, awright come in.

Two young black kids come in, **Bad T** *and* **Duane***. They are the same
age as* **Glen***.*

Duane   Yes, Glen!

Glen   Awright man? T?

Bad T   Where de booze, boy?

Glen   You mad?

Bad T   Did yu juss call me mad?

Glen   No.

Bad T   Did the boy juss call me mad, Duane?

Duane   Musta done! Cos I heard it.

Bad T   Lesson number one, don't ever call T mad, yeah.

Glen   Awright, I'm sorry.

Bad T   S'right. So pass the booze.

Glen   I can't, man.

Bad T   Did the boy jus say he can't, Duane?

Duane   Musta done, T, cos I heard it.

Bad T   Lesson number two, don't ever say you can't, yeah?

Glen   Yeah.

Bad T   Yeah wat?

Glen   Yeah watever, I'm sorry.

Bad T   Better.

Duane   The boy learnin, T. Awright, Mark?

Bad T   Come on boy, booze! I want a Jack D and Coke.

Glen   My mum will go mad.

Bad T   Mad bitch. 'Bout she chat to me like that on the phone.

Duane (*finds a picture of* **Gina** *behind the bar*)   Rah, is that her?

Glen   Yeah, she won Landlady of the Year or summin.

Bad T   How much you have in this till?

Glen   T, don't, man.

Bad T   Did the boy juss don't, T, Duane?

Duane (*laughing*)   Musta done, cos I heard it.

Bad T   Lesson number three, never say T don't, man, yeah? Yeah? Come on?

Glen   Sorry.

Bad T   Good. I was joking anyway yer fool, chill.

Duane   Check his mum, man.

Bad T   Rah!

Duane   Ennit!

Bad T   This yer mum, boy? Fer trut?

Glen   Yeah.

Bad T   Rah!

Duane   Definitely.

Bad T   Definitely would!

Duane   Definitely!

Bad T   She like it on top, Glen?

Glen   Top of wat?

Duane *roars with laughter.*

Glen   Wat?

Bad T   She turn tricks, Glen? Yer mudda turn tricks? You know wat I mean by tricks, don't yer?

Glen   Yeah.

Bad T   So, does yer mudda turn tricks?

Glen   Yeah, you mean like card tricks right?

Duane *and* **Bad T** *carry on howling.*

Glen   Wat you saying about my mum, T?

Bad T   Nuttin, forget it, Glen, yer awright.

Duane (*looks at picture of* **Gina** *again*)   Hmmm, oh yes!

Bad T   Definitely!

Glen   Careful, man.

The boys glare at him.

My mum's in the cellar.

Bad T   Did the boy juss tell us to be careful?

Duane   Musta done, cos I . . .

Bad T   Lesson number four, never . . .

Glen   . . . Yeah I'm sorry.

Bad T   You gotta learn to relax, bredren.

Duane   Ennit.

Bad T   So wat you say, Mark?

Mark   Nuttin. Yer the one doing all the talkin.

Duane   So wass up, Mark, how come you don't come round no more?

Mark   Ask yer mum.

Bad T   Wass this?

Duane   Went out wid my mum ennit.

Bad T   Yer mum's had nuff men.

Mark   You keeping out of trouble, Tyrone?

Bad T   T! Bad T!

Mark   Listen, I used to watch yer mudda change yer nappy, so don't even bother coming to me, wid this bad T business.

Bad T   (*eyes* **Glen** *and* **Duane** *laughing*)   Wat you laughin at?

Duane   Nuttin, T.

Glen   Sorry, T.

Duane   You watchin the game today, T?

Bad T   I ain't watchin no rubbish English match. They lose at everyting.

Someone's phone goes off. All the boys reach for their pockets. But it is **Mark***'s that is ringing.*

Mark   Sorry, boys. (*Answers.*) Hi, Karen, wass up? Nuh, he ain't here yet. I don't know, hold up a minute. (*Walks over to a discreet part of the bar.*) Yeah, go on.

Bad T   Rah, Glen, so thass yer phone?

Glen   Smart ennit?

Duane   Smarter than yours, T.

Bad T   Let me see. (*Examines it.*) It's light, wass the reception like?

Glen   Sharp.

Bad T   You get text yeah?

Glen   It's got everything. I can download e-mail, go on internet and that. Free voicemail.

Duane   Nice, Glen.

Glen   I know.

Mark (*to phone*)   No, I'm stayin here till he comes. I'll come back wid him. How am I suppose to know that, I juss got here.

Bad T   It's so light.

Mark   Cos yer good wid him.

Bad T   Fits into my pocket nice.

Mark   Karen, please don't start, I beg you. I'll see you later.

Bad T   Don't mess up the lining or nuttin.

Glen   Told yer.

Bad T   Sell it to me.

Glen *laughs.*

Bad T   Sell it.

Glen   Nuh, man.

Bad T   Come on.

Glen   I don't want to sell it.

Bad T   Fifteen.

Glen   No.

Bad T   Twenty.

Duane   For that? It's worth twice that . . .

Bad T   You see me talking to you, Duane?

Glen   I don't want to sell it, T.

Bad T   Wat you gonna do wid a phone like this?

Glen   Ring people and that.

Duane   Give the boy back his phone, man.

Bad T   Yeah, but it's too nice fer a white boy like him to have, best let me have it, someone who appreciates it. Look, the fool ain't even got no numbers in his phone book.

Glen   I only bought it the other day.

Bad T   Glen, has anyone, anyone at all, rang you on the phone, besides me?

Glen   No.

Bad T   Anyone ask fer yer number?

Glen   No.

Bad T   So why you reach for it, when Mark's phone rang, then?

Glen   I dunno, I juss thought . . .

Bad T   You thought wat, Glen?

Glen   I dunno, juss thought.

Bad T   I'm surprised yer brain can even do that, you thick cunt!

Duane   T, man!

Bad T   So much you sellin it to me Glen?

Glen   Nuttin.

Bad T   Nuttin, you giving it to me fer nuttin, cheers.

Glen   Hold up.

Bad T   Nice.

Glen   I don't wanna sell it.

Bad T   Twelve quid.

Glen   You said twenty a minute ago.

Bad T   Every time you say no, the price goes down. You got a nice jacket too.

Duane   T?

Bad T   Glen?

Glen   I ain't sellin it.

Bad T   Nine.

Glen   I can't.

Bad T   Eight.

Glen   I saved fer months to get it.

Bad T   Six. Keep whining, Glen. You crying now?

Glen   No.

Bad T   Fucking boy's crying, man.

Glen   I ain't.

Bad T   White boy love to cry, ennit, Duane?

Mark   Give the boy back his phone.

Bad T   Excuse me?

Mark   Give the boy back his phone, Tyrone.

Bad T   The name's T, right.

Mark   Fuck wat yer name is, give the boy back his phone.

Bad T   Here. (*Hands it back.*) Tek yer fuckin phone. (*To* **Duane**.) And you defendin him.

Duane   All I said was . . .

Bad T   Ca you love the white man. You want suck him off, ennit? (*To* **Glen**.) It was a joke, Glen, I was jokin wid you. You shouldn't carry on so, someone might juss come and tief up yer life, never mind yer mobile phone.

Gina *comes back to find* **Bad T** *and* **Duane** *behind her bar.*

Gina   Well, make yerself at home, why don't yer? And you are?

Glen   Duane and T.

Gina   Oh so, yer bad T?

Bad T   I'm big too. (*He and* **Duane** *laugh.*)

Gina   So wat are Duane, and Big T, doing behind my bar? Come on, move, out!

Bad T   You mind?

Gina   No.

Bad T   Don't touch wat you can't afford.

Gina   Is that right?

Bad T   Believe.

Gina   I will do more than touch, little boy, if you don't shift.

Duane *and* **Bad T** *ogle over her again.*

Duane   Oh yeah.

Bad T   Definitely.

Gina   You wish.

Bad T   When you lass have black in you?

Mark   Hey! Tek yer friend and go home, Tyrone.

Bad T   You my dad?

Mark   No, but I can call him. Do you want him chasin you round the estate wid his leather belt again?

Bad T (*sees* **Duane** *giggling*)   Wat you laughin at? Come!

Duane   Later, Glen.

Bad T   Yeah, go kiss yer wife goodbye!

Glen   Hold up.

Bad T   Well come now, if yer comin.

Gina   Where do you think yer going?

Glen   Yer shamin me, Mum.

Gina   I'll do more than shame yer, if you step one foot out of that door.

Glen   I won't be late.

Gina   You won't be back at all.

Glen   Later. (*He leaves.*)

Gina   He don't listen to a word I say. Like I ain't here. Fuckin kids.

Mark   That Tyrone come juss like his dad, too much mout.

Gina   So?

Mark   So?

Gina   What about you?

Mark   Nuttin.

Gina   How you doing, gorgeous?

Mark   Awright.

Gina   Thought you didn't drink in here no more.

Mark   I thought I'd slum it.

Gina   Cheeky sod. You on leave?

Mark   No I'm out.

Gina   What, for good?

Mark   So that was little Glen?

Gina   Little cunt, more like. He wants a slap. How's yer dad, Mark?

Mark   So, so.

Gina   I used to see him all the time down the high street, coming out of the betting shop – he would always call me over, sayin hello and that, askin if I have a boyfriend yet.

Mark   Yer still look good, Gina.

Gina   Yeah, yeah.

Mark   You still love to put yerself down. Didn't you see the way those boys were lookin at yer? Yer fit gal, deal wid it.

Gina   I know someone who will be very pleased to see you.

Mark   No, don't.

Gina   Shut up. (*Calls.*) Dad! In here a minute, I got a surprise.

Mark   Oh, look at the time.

Gina   Sit! Dad!

Jimmy (*off*)   Wat?

Gina   In here. Fuckin 'ell.

Jimmy (*approaching*)   Wat?

Gina   Look.

Jimmy   Marky boy! How you doin, you awright, son? You look it.

Mark   Cheers, Jimmy.

Jimmy   Still playing footie, I hope. Pub team are playing this mornin.

Mark   Yeah?

Jimmy   I still remember when you played for us, blindin he was, blindin! Everyone still talks about that goal you got against the Stag's Head – he ran with it, one end of the pitch to the other he was, no lie. He pissed on that goal Ryan Giggs got for Man U against Arsenal, pissed on it, well and truly pissed on it!

Gina   Yeah, Dad, cheers. Punters!

Jimmy   We'll talk sum more in a minute, son. You watchin the game?

Mark   Na.

Jimmy   Na!

Mark   I dunno.

Jimmy   Behave yerself.

Mark   We'll see.

Jimmy   Gina, buy him a drink on me. (*He leaves.*)

Gina   Yes, sir!

Mark   He ain't changed.

Gina   So, Mark?

Mark   Yes, Gina?

Gina   We gonna talk about what happened, or are you juss gonna sit there wid yer gob open?

Mark   Let's not. I'm juss looking for my brother Barry, I heard he drinks in here now.

Gina   I was wondering how long it would be before you came back. You see the door? Well, keep yer eyes on it, our pub team will be back any sec. He plays for them. You know he looks juss like you.

Mark   But I'm better lookin.

Doors swing open. **Lawrie** *and* **Lee**, *followed by* **Becks**, *come in. They do not look happy.*

Gina   Oh shit. Well, come on, how bad was it?

Lawrie   We stuffed the bastards!

The lads cheer.

Boys (*singing*)   Cheer up Duke of Yorks, oh what can it mean, to a, fat landlord bastard, and a, shit football team. (*Chant.*) King George, King George . . .

Gina   You tellin me you useless bastards won?

Becks   3–fuckin–2!

Gina   Oi, Dad, they only bloody won!

Lee   Set 'em up, Gina.

Lawrie   Oh yes, nuttin more sexier than a landlady pouring a smooth top.

Gina   Don't get out much, do yer, Lawrie?

Lawrie   I'll show yer wat I can get out.

Lee   Oi, behave yerself.

Gina   Like I'll be able to see it.

Becks   Nice one, Gina.

Lawrie   Kiss her arse while yer at it.

Gina   Well, come on then, blow by blow.

Lawrie   Played them off the field, Gina, gave 'em a fuckin lesson in football.

Becks   Fat cunts.

Lee   It's funny how those fat cunts were 2–0 up though.

Lawrie   Only cos of him, I coulda driven a bus through the amount of space he give 'em. Wants shooting.

Becks   Fuck off, Lawrie.

Lawrie   Oooh! You shoulda seen the looks on their faces at half time, Gina, every one of them, looking like their case was about to come up. Right, thass it, I thought, time for my pep talk. I rounded them all up, like this see –

He demonstrates, using **Lee** *and* **Becks**.

Lawrie   I goes, listen to me, listen to me! Passion! I wanna see some passion. We gotta help each other out, this is no good, we gotta learn to pass to each other, keep control of the ball! (*Screams.*) Look at me! Ain't we?

Lee/Becks   Yeah!

Lawrie   Who are yer?

Lee/Becks   The George.

Lawrie   Who are yer?

Lee/Becks   The George!

Lawrie   Thank you! Well, that was it then, second half, different story, I was going, keep back, keep back, chase, chase, keep the ball, keep the ball –

Lee   Thought he was gonna lose his voice.

Becks   I prayed he would lose his voice.

Lawrie   When Lee got the ball, I tell yer, I heard music, Gina. I goes to him.

Lee   Screaming down my ear he was.

Lawrie   Yer tart! I goes, go on, broth, give it a good spin, a nice crack, he places it right into the back, the goalie didn't know wat day it was. Coulda kissed him.

Lee   You did.

Lawrie *kisses him again.*

Gina   Who got the other two?

Lawrie   The black kid, wasshisface?

Becks   Barry. Useful, weren't he, Lawrie?

Lawrie   Yeah, he was good, the boy done good.

Becks   He did more than good, he won the game for us.

Lee   Good penalty-taker.

Becks   Wicked player.

Lawrie   Wicked player? Listen to him, trying to sound like a brother.

Becks   I'm juss sayin, he won the game for us.

Lawrie   Yeah I know wat he did, he's a wicked player, as you so delicately put it. But it was a team effort. He didn't juss win it by himself.

Becks   Might as well have.

Lawrie   You married to the cunt or wat? The boy did good, no need to break out into a song about it. Worry about yer own football, never mind droolin over wasshisface.

Becks   You callin me queer?

Lawrie   You got summin to hide, precious?

Gina   Ladies?

Becks   So wat about you, taking a swing at their captain.

Lawrie   Weren't my fault.

Becks   Nor was the goal.

Lee   Will you two lovebirds shut up?

Lawrie   That ref was a knob.

Becks   Now thass true.

Lawrie   That captain of theirs was committing untold fouls, not once did he get his book out.

Lee   Till you opened yer mouth.

Gina   What did he say?

Lawrie   Only the truth.

Lee   Don't tell her.

Lawrie   I accused him of not wanting to book one of his own.

Lee   Arsehole.

Lawrie   Cheers, broth.

Lee   I meant you.

Lawrie   Don't tell me you weren't thinkin it an all.

Becks   It's true. I saw them havin a right old chat afterwards.

Lawrie   They love stickin together, them lot.

Gina   Let me guess, the ref was black?

Lawrie   As soot. Never seen anything so dark.

Lee   Hold it down.

Lawrie   Awright, Mark? Long time no see. Still giving it large in Paddy Land? He lose his tongue or what?

Gina   Behave.

Lawrie   Only askin.

Gina   You've asked.

Lawrie   You know me, Gina, keep the peace.

Gina   Yeah.

Lee   She knows yer.

Lawrie   Got our seats, Gina?

Gina   Have a look.

Lawrie   Oh wass this, you put us at the back.

Gina   Jason asked first.

Lawrie   Fuck that. (*He swaps seats.*) You don't mind, do yer?

Gina   Any trouble, it's you I'm comin for.

Lawrie (*clicks on the remote, picture is blue*)   Gina, wass this, it's all blue.

Gina   Ask yer thievin mate over there.

Lawrie   Becks! You fuckin . . .

Becks   It was workin all right when I sold it to them.

Lawrie (*throws the remote at him*)   Fix it!

Lee   So how you doing, Mark?

Mark   Lee.

Lee   You on leave?

Mark   I quit.

Lee   You joke?

Mark   I had enuff.

Lee   You!

Mark   Yep.

Lee   How's yer dad?

Mark   Up and down. Heard about yours. Sorry, yeah.

Lee   S'right. Look, listen, yeah . . .

Mark   Don't.

Lee   Mark . . .

Mark   Don't.

Lawrie   Lee, over here a sec.

Lee   Wat?

Lawrie   Nuttin.

Lee   So wat you callin me for?

Lawrie   Geezer don't wanna know, mate.

Gina (*to* **Becks**)   Wat you fuckin done now?

Becks   I'm adjusting.

Gina   It's black an white. Juss give us some colour.

Becks   Awright, don't get out of yer pram over it. You reckon we'll win, Lawrie?

Lawrie   We better, restore some pride after that fuck-up in Belgium. I mean, how fuckin bad was that? The nation that gave the world football. (*Roars.*) Come on, you England!

Becks   Come on, England!

Lee   Come on!

Lawrie   2002, boys, make it happen.

Gina   Becks, Becks, stop!

Becks   Wat?

Gina   Weren't you watchin? You had it, picture, it was perfect, colour and everything, go back.

Becks *presses the remote.*

Gina   It's turned blue again.

Becks   Hold up.

The menu comes up on the screen.

Becks   Wass this?

Lawrie   It's the menu. Yer pressin the wrong button, you muppet.

Lee   Hold up, Becks?

Becks   Wat now?

Lee   Don't get arsey, I'm tryin to help you here.

Becks   Wat?

Lee   Go to services, on yer right.

Becks   I know.

Lee   Well, go on then.

Becks   Right.

Lee   Click on that. Now, scroll down to picture settings. Click on that. Contrast. Go up.

Gina   Yer going down, he said up.

Lawrie   Prat.

Lee   Up, up.

Becks   I'm going up.

Lee   Awright, yeah, thass it, stop! That'll do.

Lawrie   Finally.

Gina   Thank you, Constable.

Lee   Pleasure to be of service, Madam.

Gina   It's good to have someone here with brains.

Becks   Hey, wass keepin them?

Lawrie   They'll be here. Alan won't miss the kick-off, trust me.

Lee   You invited Alan?

Lawrie   Yeah.

Becks   I saw yer mate Darren, Lawrie, going into one about not getting a ticket for the game. Geezer's off his head. He reckons, he's gonna stand outside Wembley, give the Germans some verbal. Take them on like he did in Charleroi.

Lawrie   He shat himself in Charleroi. Ran back to the hotel before it all kicked off. It was me giving them Germans some gyp.

Lee   I didn't hear that, did I?

Lawrie   Of course not, Constable.

Becks   What you do?

Lawrie   We gave them a right spanking. We were in this caff, watching the game. One–nil up, right.

Becks (*chants*)   Shearer!

Lawrie   Right, shut up. There was this couple of Krauts sitting nearby, so juss for a laugh I goes, I gives the old Nazi salute, going like this I was. Fuckin ages I was at it, till finally I catches one of dem giving me the eyeball, I ask wat his problem was, he goes all menstrual, going on about cos they're Germans, it don't make them Nazis, blah, blah, bloody blah! I goes, awright, mate, calm yerself, you a Jew or wat?

Becks *laughs out loud.*

Lawrie   Next minute, the cunt's comin at me, comin at me wid a beer bottle. Tiny little cunt he was an'all. I goes, give us that, behave yerself. I take the bottle right off him, give him a slap, stamped on his fuckin head, shoulda seen it, I lean down to him, I goes, do I take it that yer not a Jew, then?

Lee   I didn't hear that, I am so not here.

Mark   You ain't changed.

Lawrie   Did he juss say summin?

Lee   No.

Lawrie   Oi, Mark, you say summin, mate? Mark? You found yer tongue then? Oi?

Lee Lawrie.

Lawrie I heard him say summin.

Lee No you didn't. Let's play.

Lawrie Have a day off, will yer? Yer off duty.

Gina Listen to the policeman, Lawrence.

Lawrie Awright. Well, put the money in.

The boys head for the table football. **Lee** *puts fifty pence in, a ball comes out. The brothers play against each other.*

Becks Do you know if Rob got a ticket for the match, Lawrie?

Lawrie He said he'd try. Bastard!

Lee It's all in the wrist!

Becks I thought I juss saw his face in the crowd, one of the cameras whizzed by, I'm sure it was him.

Lawrie Yeah? Give us a shout when you see him next. Oh wat?

Lee Skill, mate.

Becks You want to play doubles?

Lawrie Fuck off, yer worse than me.

Becks Come on.

Lawrie Ask our West Indian friend over there.

Becks (*to* **Mark**) You fancy a game, Mark?

Lee Leave him alone, Becks.

Mark Yeah, come, why not?

Becks I got a partner.

Lawrie Wat do you want me to do, sing? So, Marcus?

Mark Mark.

Lawrie How confident are yer?

Lee   Wat you doing?

Mark *throws down forty quid.*

Mark   This much? Best out of three?

Lee   Mark, don't.

Mark   You my dad?

Lawrie   Exactly. Mark, pay no attention to the old woman. Becks?

Becks   I'm short.

Mark   Don't worry about it.

Becks   Cheers, mate.

Lawrie   Let's play ball.

Mark   You gonna cover the bet?

Lawrie   Lee?

Lee   Oh bloody hell, Lawrie.

Lawrie   Come on.

Lee   Do I look like a cashpoint?

Lawrie   Broth? Brother!

Lee *(hands over forty quid)*   Pain in the arse.

Lawrie   Love yer! Gina, my love, bank this for us, will yer? Let's play ball! Mark, my boy, would you care to kick off?

Mark   No, you can.

Lawrie   No, yer awright, go ahead.

Mark   I said I'm awright.

Lawrie   Come on.

Mark   You start.

Lee   Will somebody.

Lawrie   Yer missin the point here, Mark.

Mark   Which is what?

Lawrie   You see, this here is my pub, my home from home as it were. You are a guest, I am the host, extending my hospitality.

Mark   I don't want it.

Lee   Fuck's sake, I'll do it.

He drops the ball, they all play. **Lee** *scores.*

Lawrie   Yes!

Becks   Shit sorry.

Mark   Don't worry.

He plays the ball. He plays like a lunatic, he is too fast for **Lawrie** *and* **Lee** *and scores.*

Mark   Yes!

Lawrie   Right, come on, Lee.

Lee *drops the ball in.* **Mark** *is just as fast, if not faster, and scores again.*

Becks   Yes!

Lawrie   Shit. Come on, Lee.

Lee   Awright!

He drops the ball again. **Mark** *is playing like a maniac now.* **Becks** *just stops and stands back and watches him.* **Mark** *scores.*

Mark   Oh yes!

Lawrie   Bollocks!

Becks   Does it hurt being that good, Mark?

Mark   Torture. Cheers, Gina. (*Collects the money from her.*)

Lawrie   You knew he was useful.

Lee   I knew you wouldn't listen.

Mark   Another please, Gina.

Gina   So you still here?

Mark   Till I see my brother.

Gina   Dad will be pleased.

Lee   Still practising?

Mark   Another time, Lee.

Lee   Gina dumped me as well, you know.

Mark   I don't care about that.

Lee   Sod yer, then.

Mark   Right on.

Door opens. **Phil**, **Jason** *and* **Alan** *enter. Loud cheering, singing, except* **Alan**, *who walks in coolly, standing between them.* **Lawrie**, **Becks** *and* **Lee** *join their mates in the singing.*

Boys   We're on our way, we are Kev's twenty-two, hear the roar, of the red, white and blue, this time, more than any other, this time, we're gonna find a way, find a way to get it on, time, get it on together.

Gina   Shall we keep it down, gents? Hi, Phil.

Phil   Awright, Gina.

Gina   So how's life in Watford?

Phil   Sweet as.

Becks   He'll be following their team next.

Phil   Bollocks.

Becks   Giving Elton John a tug.

Phil   Shut it, Becks.

Boys (*sing*)   Don't sit down, with Elton around, or you might get a penis up yer arse!

Gina   Now, now, boys, not in front of the lady.

Alan   It's all right, Gina, I'll keep them in line. (*To screen.*) Come on, lads, got a lot of living up to do.

Phil   We had 'em in June.

Alan   Romania had us in June. (*To* **Gina**.) Where's yer dad?

Gina (*shouts*)   Dad? Like yer haircut, Phil.

Phil   Yeah?

Gina   Yeah, very David Beckham. Suits yer.

The boys start teasing **Phil** *regarding* **Gina**.

Phil   Behave yerselves.

Becks (*watching the screen*)   Commentary's started.

Jason (*roars*)   Come on, lads.

Phil   Come on, you England!

Lawrie *and* **Lee** *join in the roar.* **Jimmy** *appears to get some crisps.*

Jimmy   Wat?

Gina   Yer little friend's here.

Jimmy   Awright, Alan?

Alan   James. Watchin the game?

Jimmy   Be right wid yer, juss serving.

Alan   Lawrie, my boy. Good result today, well played.

Lawrie   You remember my kid brother, Lee.

Alan   The policeman – you all right, son?

Lee   Yep.

Alan   Spitting image of yer old man you are. Still a PC?

Lawrie   Detective Constable now, if you don't mind, movin to Sutton.

Lee   Lawrie –

Lawrie   Shut up, I don't know why yer keepin it a secret, I'm proud of yer. I kept tellin him it would work out for him, but he never believes me. The state he was in last year.

Alan   State?

Lawrie   Got stabbed.

Alan   Nasty.

Lawrie   Yeah, some coon. It happened at a rave, weren't it, Lee?

Lee   Will you shut up?

Lawrie   He didn't hear, like I care.

Alan   Easy, son.

Boys (*chant*)   ENGLAND, ENGLAND, ENGLAND! (*Etc.*)

Becks   Come on, Rob, where are yer?

Jason   Wat, is he there?

Becks   He was in the crowd a second ago.

Phil   How did he get in? He's banned.

Lawrie   You think that'll stop Rob? They tried to stop us going into France for '98, we were there though, despite all the efforts and a huge operation by the boys in blue to keep us away. Oops, sorry Lee, you didn't hear that. We were there though, oh, we were so there.

Jason   You there when the trouble kicked off?

Lawrie   The second Batty missed that penalty, I knew it was gonna kick off. It was fuckin war on the streets. Argys, Krauts, coppers, didn't fuckin matter. We were England!

Alan   Thinking went right out of the window.

Lawrie   Least we were winnin that one.

Alan   You got arrested and thrown in a French cell, you daft sod. Never fight a battle you can't win.

Jason   Wat was Batty doin taking a penalty anyhow?

Mark   Jase?

Jason   Awright, Mark?

Mark   Where's my brother? He was playin today?

Alan   You're Barry's brother?

Mark   Yes.

Alan   You should be proud of him, that boy is useful.

Mark   He ain't a boy.

Alan   Easy.

Mark   Where is he?

Jason   He walked.

Mark   While you all drove?

Alan   There wasn't enough room. I had a lot of stuff in the back. I'm a painter and decorator. It was hard getting those two muppets in. We drew straws.

Mark   And he got the short one?

Alan   Yes, he did. What's his problem?

Mark   You can talk to me.

Alan   No need to fly off, son.

Mark   Where's my brother?

Barry, *comes in, dancing and singing (New Order's 'World in Motion'). He makes a right show of it, parading himself in front of the lads who are egging him on.* **Barry** *has the flag of St George painted on both cheeks.*

After singing the final verse, he is joined in the chorus by the boys.

Phil   Barry, over here!

Barry *goes over to the boys. One by one, they take turns rubbing or kissing his bald head.*

Barry   Anyone else?

Alan   Yeah, over here, boy. (*Rubs his head.*)

Phil   Good boy.

Jason   Fuckin won it for us.

Barry   Thank you, thank you, thank you. (*Sees* **Mark**.)
Awright, bruv?

Mark   Can I talk to you?

Barry   Game's gonna start.

Mark   Won't take long.

Jason   Got yer seat here, Baz.

Barry   Cheers, Jase.

*The teams line up to hear the national anthems. The German one plays
first. The lads boo and jeer.*

Boys (*to the tune of 'Go West'*)   Stand up, if you won the war!
Stand up, if you won the war, stand up, if you won the war . . .

Gina   Feet off the seats, if you please.

*The English national anthem is played. The boys sing along. Some jump
on the table,* **Gina** *protests. They all cheer at the end.*

Boys (*chant*)   ENGLAND! ENGLAND! ENGLAND!

Alan   Come on, lads.

Lawrie   Let's fuckin have some!

Alan   Lawrence? About wat we spoke about – yer in.

Lawrie   Cheers.

Lee (*approaches*)   Wat was that?

Lawrie   Nosey.

Game kicks off. Boys cheer and applaud.

Mark   Barry?

Barry   Later, Mark – come on, pull up a chair.

Phil   You tell him, boy.

Mark (*grabs him*)   Come here!

Barry   Hey!

Mark Excuse us!

He ushers his brother into the Gents, where they start to bicker.

Becks Wass up there?

Lawrie Must be a black thing.

Phil Come on, you England!

The boys join **Phil***'s roar. Lights up on the Gents.*

Barry I'm missin the start here.

Mark Wat was that? Dancin like sum spaz, lettin them rub yer head like a genie's lamp.

Barry They do it at every match, for luck. It's a laugh.

Mark Wipe that shit off yer face.

Barry Don't come down here and start, Mark.

Mark You think I'm here by choice? I feel ill juss bein here. I can't wait to go home so I can have a wash.

Barry Go home then. Let me watch the match.

Mark Karen said you ain't bin home fer weeks, wass that about? Too busy to see yer own dad?

Barry You come to take me back?

Mark He's askin for yer.

Barry I ain't seein him.

Mark Show sum respect.

Barry For that mess that lies in bed all day? That ain't my dad, why can't he hurry up and die?

Mark Fuckin little . . .

Barry Karen feels the same way, you as well. You love to act high and mighty now yer back, where were you when he was gettin sick?

Mark Look, let's chat when we get home, yeah?

Barry   I'm watchin the game.

Mark   Where you get that cut on yer neck?

Barry   Romanian fan. Charleroi.

Mark   You were at Charleroi? Fuck's sake.

Barry   Shoulda seen wat I did to him. (*Demonstrates.*) Glassed him right up.

Mark   Why don't you get a tatoo of the Union Jack while yer at it?

Barry *rolls up his shirt. He has a tattoo of the British Bulldog on his lower back.*

Barry   I didn't even pass out. Almost as good as yours, I reckon.

Mark   Wat are you doin to yerself?

Barry   Nuttin you wouldn't do, once.

Mark   I don't want Dad going thru this shit again.

Barry   Fuck off back to the army.

Mark   I'm outta the army, little man, for good.

Barry   Lose yer bottle again, Mark?

Mark   Yer comin home.

Barry   No.

Mark   I'll follow you all day if I have to.

Barry   Do it.

Mark   Kid . . .

Barry   I ain't a fuckin kid no more! You don't understand!

Mark   I don't understand?

Barry   I'm missin it.

Mark   You think yer a badman now, cos you've had a couple of rucks, kicked a few heads? You've got no idea, son. When yer all alone with a gang of them, havin to fight 'em off by yourself, getting the shit kicked outta yer for yer trouble, you get back to me. It's bollocks, kid. It's their bollocks.

The boys stamp on the floor as they chant to the tune of The Great Escape. **Barry** *leaves the loo to watch the match with his mates. He joins in with the chant. The screen turns blue again. The boys protest.*

Gina   Becks, you stupid . . .

Becks   I'll fix it.

Gina   Keep yer bloody hands off.

Lee   Giss it.

Lawrie   Come on, broth.

Lee   Shut up.

He sorts out the contrast. The colour picture comes back. The boys applaud.

Phil   Nice.

Becks   Juss needs a bit of TLC now and then.

Gina   I want my money back.

Phil   Come on, England!

Boys (*chant*)   ENGLAND! ENGLAND! ENGLAND! . . .

Becks (*mocks*)   Southgate in the middle though.

Phil   When did Cole score last?

Mark   When did he last get a full game?

Gina (*approaches*)   Come on, boys, bunch up.

The boys get all excited by **Gina** *joining them. Cheers, wolf whistles etc.*

Gina   All barks, no bites. You stayin then, Mark?

Mark   Yeah. Might as well.

Jason   Lampard should be playing.

Phil   An Hammer playing, behave yerself.

Jimmy Shut yer face, Philip. You juss bring on yer bloody Chelsea at Upton Park, you'll bloody know it then.

Mobile phone rings. It's **Becks***'s.*

Becks Hello. Awright, Rob!

Jason (*shouts*) Robbie, yer cunt!

Lawrie Yer wanker!

Becks Yer hear that? I said did yer hear that?

Lawrie Where is he? (*Shouts.*) Where are yer, yer cunt!

Becks He's there!

Jason Wembley?

Becks Yes, Jase, fuckin Wembley! (*To phone.*) Wat now? He goes there's a camera comin into view, he's gonna wave at us.

Phil He's there, fuckin 'ell!

They all cheer and wave.

Becks We see yer, yer there.

They all see Rob from the screen; the boys scream and cheer louder. **Phil** *pulls his trousers down and moons at the screen.*

Becks Rob, Phil is only showin you his arse.

Gina (*to* **Jimmy**) No trouble, eh?

Jimmy Philip, no more arse!

The boys roar with laughter as they see Rob mooning back at them.

Lawrie He's only moonin back at us!

Jason Yer wanker!

Becks Ring me at half-time, yer nutter!

Lawrie I tell yer, if we lose again, it's gonna kick off in there.

Kelly (*off*) Jimmy?

Jimmy Kelly needs some help, Gina.

Gina You better get back there.

Jimmy (*shouts*) I'll be there in a sec.

Gina Dad?

Jimmy Fuck's sake!

The boys laugh as **Jimmy** *has to leave.*

Yeah, yeah, up yours.

Becks Germans playing three at the back?

Barry Looks like it.

Jason Yes, come on, Owen.

Becks Fuck!

Lee Good run, though.

Barry He's a fast one.

Alan Yeah, but then he lost it.

Jason Nice one, Adams, make him eat dirt.

Lawrie He's given away a free kick, yer sap.

Phil Watch the post, watch the fuckin post!

Jason Good one, Le Saux.

Becks Doin summin right for once.

Jason Leave him.

Becks (*acting camp*) Oooh! (*Blows* **Jason** *a kiss.*)

Jason Fuck off.

Gina Nice control by Cole, eh?

Lawrie Yeah, but he's all mouth, no delivery, him.

Mark Cos no one gives him a chance.

Lawrie Cos he never fuckin scores.

Mark   Shearer played nine games without scoring for England, nine! Didn't stop Venables pickin him.

Lawrie   Cole ain't Shearer.

Mark   He's never bin given a chance to be Shearer.

Barry   Lawrie's right.

Mark   Wat you know?

Barry   Watch him. He needs three or four chances to score a goal, Shearer only needed one.

Mark   He got forty-one goals in one season when he was with Newcastle, how many's he's put in for Man U? Wat do you want? Since when is a striker judged on how many chances he gets, leave me alone.

Phil   Southgate, you useless piece of shit.

Jason *takes out horn and blows on it; everyone jumps.*

Becks   Jase!

Phil   'Kin 'ell.

Jason   Juss tryin to whip up a bit of excitement.

Gina   I'll whip it up yer arse.

Alan   Nice one, Scholes.

Lawrie   Come on, Scholes.

Barry   Get it up.

They sigh as Scholes loses the ball to German player Ballack. Scholes tugs him. Ballack falls. Free kick.

Becks   Wat!

Phil   Hamman won't score.

Barry   He plays for Liverpool, ennit.

Hamman shoots from the free kick. He scores. German fans cheer. The boys are stunned.

Phil   Oh wat!

Jason   Nice one, Baz, yer jinxed it.

Barry   Move!

Jason   He did.

Lee   Wat difference it makes, he still scored.

The German manager, Rudi Voller, is celebrating.

Lawrie   Fuck off, you German cunt!

Boys (*chant*)   YER DIRTY GERMAN BASTARD! YER
DIRTY GERMAN BASTARD!

Lawrie   Jase, ring Rob, tell him to give one of them Krauts
a slap from me.

Alan   There's no point in taking it out on them.

Lawrie   Oh, come on.

Alan   We should have had a red shirt in front of the ball.
It weren't a strong kick, Seaman should have got that.

Barry   We were well asleep at the back. Hamman saw a
chance, he took it.

Alan   Too right he took it. The boy's right.

Phil   Check Keegan's face.

Becks   Yeah, you better be worried.

Jason   He was never cut out to be manager.

Barry   Ain't wat you said when he got the job, going on
about him being the people's choice.

Jason   I never said that.

Barry   Lie!

Gina   Can we not bury them yet, please.

England are awarded a free kick. Beckham lines up to take it.

Lee   Oh yes!

Lawrie   Come on, Beckham.

Phil   Get it in the box, please.

Jason   Lets have some more reds in there!

Barry   And leave them well exposed at the back, good call, Jase.

Jason   Piss off, Barry.

Barry   Ooh, handbag.

Jason   Scores a couple this mornin, and he thinks he's the dog's bollocks.

Beckham crosses the ball. It's headed back.

Gina   Get it back. And Phil?

Phil   Yeah?

Gina   Stop lookin at my tits.

The boys laugh as they tease **Phil***, calling him a pervert etc.*

Phil   I weren't.

Jimmy (*approaching*)   How goes it?

Becks   Phil's bin looking at Gina's tits.

Phil   I weren't, Jimmy, I swear to God.

Jimmy   You'll be prayin to God for your life, mate, if you step out. (*Sees.*) Oh Jesus. One–nil!

Mark   Hamman scored a blinder.

Lawrie   You a Kraut-lover now?

Alan   Easy, Lawrence

Lawrie   It was a poxy free kick.

Mark   Watever.

Lawrie   No watever about it, boy.

Mark   Shut yer hole.

Lawrie   Shut my wat, wass he say?

Lee   Yer missin the match.

Gina   Are we happy over there?

Lawrie   Sweet as.

Gina   Good.

The Germans are on the attack. Bierhof is passed the ball. He is in an excellent position to score.

Becks   Shit.

Jason   Flag's up.

Barry   Offside!

Phil   Come on, England!

Jimmy   They wanna stop playin wid themselves!

Cole has the ball, he makes a run.

Phil   Come on, Cole.

Jason   Yes.

Barry   Free kick.

Jason   Which cunt got him?

Gina   Rehmar. Do you know any other words apart from cunt, Jase?

Beckham lines up for another free kick

Alan   Come on, Beckham.

Gina   I don't care how he talks, he is gorgeous.

Jason   He'll score.

Barry   Got a crystal ball, Jase?

Beckham shoots, he misses.

You were sayin?

Jason   It was on target.

Barry   Yeah, look on the bright side.

Jason   Wass yer problem?

Barry   I'm havin a laugh.

Jason   Leave it out.

Barry   Or wat?

Gina   Girls!

Lawrie   Come on, Owen!

Alan   Ooh, unlucky, son.

Phil   That fuckin coach of theirs looks like Terry McDermott.

Jimmy   He was a good player, that Voller.

Alan   How many goals he got when he was playin, Jimmy?

Jimmy   'Bout forty-seven. Class player.

Lawrie   For a Kraut.

Alan   Nothing wrong with admiring the enemy once in a while.

Phil   Come on, boys.

Barry   England!

Jason   They wanna take fucking Cole off.

Mark   Why?

Jason   Ain't pullin his weight.

Mark   He ain't alone.

Jason   I'm juss stating my opinion.

Mark   Funny how he's the only black player on the pitch.

The boys protest at that remark.

Gina   Come off it, Mark.

Mark   All I said, it was funny.

Jason   If thass wat I meant, that's wat I woulda said.

Mark   Why him?

Jason   He's playin shit.

Barry   Yer talkin shit.

Mark   Thank you.

Barry   Both of yer.

Mark   Hey, easy.

Jason   Paranoia.

Mark   I'm done,

He goes to the Gents. **Lee** *follows.*

Lawrie   Where you going?

Lee   For a slash.

Jason   Wass yer brother's problem? He sayin I'm a racist?

Barry   I don't know wat he's doing.

Jason   Wanker.

Lights on in the Gents.

Lee   You don't even like Andy Cole. You told me once, you can't fart loud enough to describe how much you hate Man U, and anyone who plays for them.

Mark   Is it?

Lee   So wat gives? Did you hear that the Post Office recalled their Man U treble commemorative stamps, people couldn't figure out which side to spit on? Wat do Man U fans use for birth control? Their personalities. A man meets up with his mate and sees that his car is a total write-off, all covered with leaves, grass, branches, dirt and blood. He asks his mate, wat happened to yer car? The friend replies, well, I ran over David Beckham. Bloke goes, that explains the blood, but what about the leaves, the grass, and branches and dirt. The geezer says . . .

Mark   . . . he tried to escape by runnin through the park.

He tries hard not to laugh, but gives in a little. He then heads out.

Lee   So wat was that with Jason?

Mark   He's a prick.

Lee   I know he's a prick, he ain't racist.

Mark   Like you?

Lee   Yeah, gwan, Mark, tell half the story.

Mark   Wass there to tell, yer Lawrie's brother.

Lee   You know I ain't like him.

Mark   Wat you gonna do about Alan?

Lee   He ain't committed an offence.

Mark   Not yet.

Lee   If he does.

Mark   When.

Lee   I'll have him. So wass this about you quittin the army?

Mark   They didn't like the colour of my eyes.

Lee   Oh, come on.

Mark   Don't worry yerself.

Lee   I'm gettin married, next month. Her name's Vicky. She's nice, fit.

Mark   Nice one.

Lee   Come to the wedding. Please

Lights up in the bar.

Barry   Don't tell me we don't have players who know how to pass, it's like we're scared of the ball or summin.

Lawrie (*aside*)   Them and this 'we'.

Alan   You enjoy supporting our boys then, son?

Barry   They're my boys too.

Lawrie   Armchair supporter.

Barry   I bin to Wembley eight times, I never saw you there.

Alan   Wat was yer first game?

Barry   1990, against Yugoslavia. Mark took me.

Alan   Two—one. Bryan Robson, both goals.

Lawrie   Fuck this!

Lee (*approaches*)   Where you going? (*Follows.*)

Lawrie *heads for the pool table. He wipes off the names from the board.*

Lee   You can't do that.

Lawrie (*points at his own face*)   Bothered?

Lee   We still got the second half.

Lawrie   They're gonna walk over us, like everyone else!

Lee   Calm down.

Lawrie   Fuckin taking it! Same old shit, like Belgium.

Lee   You give up too easily.

Lawrie   So do they. Why do they always do this to us? I wish I was there, give them Kraut bastards summin to laugh about.

Lee   Enough.

Lawrie   They've got no heart, Lee. We give 'em ours, every single game, and we get fuck-all back. If those cunts can't do it on the pitch, we can, we will! We're England!

Lee   Yer a prick.

Lawrie   Yer not playing?

Lee   Fuck off.

Alan (*approaches*)   Set 'em up, Lawrie.

Lee *blocks* **Alan***'s path.*

Alan   Help you, son?

Lee   Leave him alone.

Alan   Spitting image of yer old man.

Lee   Are you deaf?

Lawrie   Shut up, Lee.

Alan   You and I should have a drink. (*Goes over to* **Lawrie**.) Tragic ennit?

Lawrie   Ninety minutes, Alan, to forget about all the shit out there, and they can't even do that.

Alan   Your dad would be spinning.

They play pool. **Mark** *is at the bar with* **Gina**, *who is pulling him a pint.*

Gina   You calm down? Arsehole. You hate Andy Cole.

Mark   I know, I'm sorry. Is Barry behavin himself?

Gina   Rowdy as the rest of them, nuttin I can't handle. He's all right.

Mark   He's stupid. Loves to get led round all the time. The amount of times Mum and Dad had to go to his school, cos of him.

Gina   Like you weren't like that as well.

Mark   He should listen to wat I'm sayin then, ennit?

Gina   You and Lee still ain't talkin. Bit silly, ennit?

Mark   I knew you'd dump him.

Gina   He's gettin married.

Mark   He said.

Gina   He's brought her in a few times. Posh bit, really nice. Daddy owns a computer company.

Mark   You coulda called me.

Gina   And get back wid you, yer mad! I hated myself.

Mark   Don't.

Gina   You two were like that. I got between yer.

Mark   Writing was on the wall long before.

He rejoins the boys. **Glen** *comes into the pub; he has been beaten up. He is not wearing his jacket. He tries to sneak in without being seen.*

Jimmy   Glenny boy, get yer arse over here, make yourself useful, clear up some glasses.

Glen   I ain't doin nuttin.

Jimmy   You'll do as yer told, I ain't soft like yer bleedin mum. (*Clocks his face.*) Watcha run into?

Glen   Don't worry yerself.

Jimmy   Gina?

Glen   No.

Jimmy   Over here.

Gina   Jesus! You bin fighting again? Wass the matter wid you? And where's yer jacket? Where's yer fuckin jacket?

Glen   Gone.

Gina   Gone where?

Glen   Juss gone.

Gina   Well, you better find out where's it gone, and get it back.

Glen *winces when* **Gina** *grabs his arm.*

Jimmy   Oh Christ, she barely touched yer.

Gina   Glen?

Glen   He took my jacket and my phone, ennit? Cos he liked 'em.

Gina   Who?

Glen   Tyrone. Bad T.

Gina   That fuckin little black kid?

Jimmy   You let him take it off yer? You didn't even fight back?

Alan   All right there, Jimmy?

Jimmy   Should be ashamed of yerself.

Alan   Jimmy?

Jimmy   Some fuckin little black kid has had a pop at my boy.

Gina   Little bastard.

Lawrie   Who are they?

Jimmy (*to* **Glen**)   Stop cryin.

Glen   I ain't.

Jimmy   Only got a scratch, stand up straight.

Gina   Dad?

Jimmy   Teach you how to fight, then you can go back, sort 'em out.

Gina   Leave him alone. I'm gonna kill the little cunt.

Mark   You mean black cunt? (*To* **Barry**.) You gettin this?

Gina   Come on, Mark, they were a couple wrong uns, you saw 'em yerself. Even if I was thinkin it, can you blame me? Wass the matter wid you, look at his face.

Jimmy   A poxy scratch.

Gina   Would they have nicked his stuff if he was black?

Lawrie   No.

Lee   Where you goin?

Lawrie   Find this kid.

Lee   Lawrie!

Alan   I'll go.

Lee   You stay. (*Leaves.*)

Becks   You ever seen a more shittier pass than that?

Phil   Come on!

Barry   England! (*Screams.*) Come on, you England!

Mark *sits alongside his brother*

Barry   You still here?

Mark   Juss watchin the game.

Barry   So wat about Dad?

Mark   Karen's lookin after him.

Barry   You don't want to go back home any more than me.

Lawrie *and* **Lee** *come in; they have* **Duane***.*

Duane   I was comin to give 'em back, right.

Lawrie   Yeah.

Duane   Move, right!

Lawrie   Mouthy little . . .

Duane   Glen, tell 'em, man, it weren't me, it was T, right?

Lawrie (*slaps his head*)   You want another?

Mark   Hey, you don't have to hit him.

Lee (*stands between them*)   Let's juss chill, yeah.

Mark   Let the boy go.

Lee   I'm handling it, Mark.

Jimmy   Go on, son, game's still playin.

Mark   Fuck the game!

Lee (*to* **Duane**)   Where's the phone?

Duane *hands it over*

Duane   I was gonna give it back, I told T – he loves to go too far sometimes, but he don't listen.

Lee   You scared of him?

Duane   Yeah.

Lee   So how come you got the phone and jacket off him?

Duane   I dunno. I juss did.

Lawrie   Lying.

Lee   On yer way.

Duane   Glen, I'm sorry, yeah.

Lawrie   He said out!

Duane   Fuck off!

Lawrie *grabs the boy and slings him out.*

Mark   Fuckin . . .

Lawrie   Come on, come on!

Lee   It's over. (*To* **Lawrie**.) Leave it, Lawrie.

Mark   You big it up now ennit?

Jimmy (*to* **Glen**)   See wat trouble you've caused? Wouldn't happen if you stick up for yerself.

Gina   Dad, if you don't stop goin on at him, I'm gonna shove this beer glass into yer face! (*To* **Mark**.) And you, sit down and watch the game.

Alan (*aside*)   Rivers of blood.

Gina   Go upstairs, Glen, clean yer face. Alan, I appreciate your trade, it's always nice to see yer, but I've told you before, I don't want to hear that kind of talk in my pub. Leave that England-for-whites bollocks outside.

Phil   Fuck's sake!

Jason   Will somebody please score!

Alan   Come on, Jimmy, you know what I'm talking about.

Gina   Excuse me, it's my name above that door.

Alan   I'm sorry, babe, I didn't mean to upset you.

Gina   Then don't say it.

Alan   It's not just me, darling. I've got nothing against the coloureds myself, but even you have to admit we've got a problem here. There are too many different races all trying to fit into the same box, how is that supposed to work? Now they've got our kids talking like them. It's no wonder you feel the same.

Gina   I do not.

Alan   But I just heard you call that kid a black cunt.

Gina   Cos they beat up my son.

Becks   Fuckin chase it!

Alan   Come on, Gina.

Becks   Chase!

Alan   They think we're all racists anyway.

Becks   Come on!

Alan   'All white people are racists.' I heard this black geezer say it once, dead clever. We are racists. We are white, he says. Our history, our culture, our jobs, people on TV, it's all white, if not predominantly. It's not by coincidence It's by design. Being white is the norm. It always has been. We are the norm. You should have heard him.

Gina   Well, he's wrong.

Alan   Is he?

Jimmy   You were barely on solids when Enoch said his piece, Gina – they were lining to carve him up.

Gina   Good.

Jimmy   All he said was the truth.

Gina   And you agree, you stupid old git.

Jimmy   Look at all the trouble we've got now, it's those fucking black kids from that estate that are causing it all. You know that. I can handle the older blacks, Mark's dad used to drink in here, blindin fella. But these young ones really know how to push it, mouthing off, carryin on like the world owes them a favour, bollocks.

The boys watching the match let out a huge sigh.

Jason   That was so close.

Phil   Nice one, Seaman.

Becks   Not bad for an Arsenal man.

Jimmy   Then there's the asylum seekers.

Gina   Oh, Dad.

Jimmy   You can't deny it, they're everywhere.

Gina   Where, Dad? Where? Down the high street, in here? Where? I don't see 'em.

Lawrie   Tucked away in their nice council homes.

Gina   I'm not hearing this, Lee?

Lee   Leave me out of it.

Lawrie   He knows it's true.

Lee   You a mind-reader?

Lawrie   I'm yer brother.

Jimmy   It's in the papers, love.

Gina   Yeah, and those papers lie on a regular basis when it comes to the likes of us. Throw in a pair of tits and they've got you hypnotised. Can you not prove their point, please.

Alan   Gina, love, I don't read papers, I haven't picked one up in years. I read books, and I'm tellin you, it's amazing what you read. Pages of it, reams of it, history, telling you, making valid points that the blacks, the non-whites, have absolutely nothing in common with the Anglo-Saxon Celtic culture.

Gina   The what?

Alan   If they want to practise their black culture and
heritage, then they should be allowed to do it in their own part
of the world. By all means.

Gina   So whites are superior to blacks?

Alan   Yes.

Gina   Bollocks.

Alan   Consider this: the blacks lived side by side with the
Egyptians for thousands of years, only about twenty miles of
sand separated them. When the Egyptians came into contact
with them, they hadn't even invented the wheel, which the
Egyptians had thousands of years ago, they couldn't even copy it.

Gina   Maybe they didn't need it.

Alan   What has the black man done in the world?

Gina   Thass it! (*Goes back to watching the game.*)

Alan   I'll tell you. When the British and European powers
colonised Africa, the colonies had a high standard of
civilisation; when the decolonialisation came round, we left
these countries economically sound with good administrative
government. As soon as the whites left, those blacks are killing
each other. Now they've got some of the poorest countries in
the world. That's how capable the blacks are of running their
own countries and looking after themselves. You look at the
rest of the black hemisphere, the Caribbean, rotten with
poverty, half of them, now we gave them the means to run
their countries efficiently, but we're still pumping aid into these
countries to keep them afloat. If they can't even live with each
other, why should we be expected to live with them as well?
Look at us, we won the war militarily, but we lost it in real
terms; see the Germans, Japanese, the two strongest economies
in the world, because their countries had been so heavily
bombed that money had to be pumped in to rebuild their
industries. They've managed it, why couldn't the blacks whose
countries weren't even destroyed? Why do we always have to
keep giving in to their begging bowls? Money which we could

do with ourselves, never mind how the poor blacks are suffering around the world.

Lee *gives* **Alan** *a sarcastic slow hand-clap.*

Alan   You know, Lee, you remind me of this copper I met once, he told me about this black geezer who was parking his car, music blaring out from his speakers. My mate the copper asks the geezer to turn the music down, neighbours bin complaining. The geezer starts effing and blinding at him, carrying on like my mate was putting the chains back on him. Anything like that happen to you, Lee?

Lawrie   All the time.

Lee   Why don't you tell him my whole life? (*Goes back to the game.*)

Lawrie (*follows*)   They got no respect, Lee, you know that.

Lee   Yer gonna lecture them about respect, Lawrie?

Jason   We're gonna be two–nil down.

Becks   We need a goal.

Mark   Doubt it somehow.

Barry   No ideas, not one creative mind.

Jason   Where's Gazza when you need him?

Mark   Gazza of old.

Sharon, **Duane**'s *mum, comes bursting in.*

Sharon   Which one of you bastards hurt my boy?

Jimmy   Gina?

Sharon   Which one of you touch him?

Gina   You wanna calm down please, love.

Sharon   Move!

Gina   Do it, or leave my pub.

Sharon Yer lucky I don't bring the police 'bout you rough up my son!

Gina Yer son nicked my boy's phone.

Sharon Weren't him.

Gina He told you that?

Sharon I said it weren't him. You didn't even give him a chance to explain, you tek one look, see his face, thass it! Hey, don't walk away from me, yer racist bitch!

Gina Wat did you say?

Sharon Yer deaf?

Alan Yer boy was shoutin the odds.

Sharon You can shut yer mout as well. I bet it was you.

Lee Calm down, love.

Sharon Let go of my arm.

Lee I said calm down.

Sharon You the police?

Lee Yes. Now calm yerself down, before I arrest yer.

Sharon Oi, bitch, I ain't finished wid you. Who did it?

Gina Get her out of my face.

Lee Mark, help us out here.

Mark No.

Sharon Don't look yer nose down on me, right!

Gina Get out, you silly cow.

Sharon Come mek me, I'll tear out yer fucking eye.

Lee Leave it!

Sharon *strikes out at* **Lee**. **Lawrie** *screams out his brother's name.* **Lee** *restrains her by twisting her arm behind her back.* **Sharon** *shrieks in pain.*

Lawrie   You awright, son?

Lee   Yes!

Lawrie   You sure?

Mark   Lee!

Lee   You had yer chance, back off.

Phil   Wass goin on?

Becks (*sees the commotion*)   Jesus! Yer brother, Baz.

Barry   So wat?

Mark   Lee, get off her man.

Lee   I told you, Mark.

Sharon   Bitch!

Lee   Jimmy, call the police.

Act Two

Same location as Act One.

Jason, **Barry**, **Becks** *are watching the game. It is a few minutes into the second half.* **Phil** *is watching the commotion going on outside the window.*

Barry I'd give Posh Spice a fucking good seeing-to, I would. Fuck her till she screams. I'd strip off all her clothes, her damp and sticky knickers, I'd lay her down on the floor, frig her pussy with my fingers, rubbing away at her clit, till she had an orgasm. Then I'd give her a fuck, long lingering fuck. And she'll take it cos she's juicy and sexed up. I'll find out if she takes it up the arse. I'll do it. You hear me, Beckham? Thass wat I'm gonna do to yer fucking wife, if you don't score some goals!

Jason Easy, Barry.

Barry He's gettin on my nerves.

Becks Ain't he carryin sum injury?

Phil Left knee.

Becks I bet he's thinkin about Man U. Playing for England don't mean nuttin to them any more.

Barry Three lions on the shirt.

Becks You'd rather see Man U lose, and England win?

Barry We ain't watchin Man U, we're watchin England. When England play, Man U don't exist. Bloody money they're on.

Phil More police out there, they're tellin that Sharon to shut it.

Jason Just cart her off, the mad bitch.

Phil She's got sum mouth.

Barry (*chants*) ENGLAND! ENGLAND!

Phil   Now Mark's gettin stuck in, he's gonna get nicked an all, if he ain't careful.

Barry   Come on!

Phil   Now she's mouthin off at Mark.

Jason   Gina?

Phil   Sharon! Tellin him he don't need his help. Barry, shouldn't you be out there?

Barry   ENGLAND!

Phil   Baz!

Barry   Wat?

Phil   He's your brother, you should be backing him up.

Barry   I'm watchin the game.

Becks   You ain't gonna miss anything.

Barry   So why are you still here then?

Jason   Cos we follow England.

Barry   Wat you tryin to say, Jase?

Jason   Nuttin.

Barry   I'm not white enuff for England?

Jason   Oh, behave yerself.

Barry   Is it?

Jason   You lot need to chill out.

Barry   Black people.

Jason   Awright, yeah! Black people. Going off on one all the time. Whenever someone says the slightest thing. All yer doing is pissing people off.

Barry   All I'm doing is watching the match.

Jason   So watch it! 'Kin ell.

Becks   Awright, boys, come on, let's bring out the peace pipe. Look, Kieron Dyer's on, he might do summin. (*Goes behind the bar.*) Who wants a drink, Phil? Come on, free round.

Phil   Awright quick, top this up.

Barry   Sharon is nuttin but a mouthy cow. She wants to get nicked, thass her grief.

Becks   Yes, Baz, watever, mate, calm yerself.

Barry   I am calm.

Becks   Good.

Barry (*chants*)   ENGLAND!

Jimmy *and* **Gina** *come back in.*

Gina   Crazy bitch.

Jimmy   Awright, love.

Gina   She's a fuckin loon. (*To* **Jason** *and* **Barry**.) Get yer bloody feet off my seats.

Jimmy (*to* **Becks**)   Settling in? Get yer arse out of there. Yer a thievin little bastard, Julian, juss like yer old man.

Becks   I was gonna pay.

Jimmy   Too right you'll pay, how much you had, you little – ?

Jason   He ain't had much, Jimmy, I swear. Come on, whose round, Phil?

Phil   Na.

Jason   Yer as tight-arsed as Becks, you.

Barry   I'll get 'em in.

Jason   You got the lass one.

Barry   I don't mind.

Becks   Yeah, Jase, shut up, same again please, Barry my man.

Phil   And me.

Barry *goes to the bar.*

Gina   Sorry for wat I said. That Sharon juss wound me up. You know me, I ain't got a problem with nobody.

Barry   It's awright.

Gina   Yer brother won't see it that way.

Barry   I ain't my brother.

Gina   OK.

Barry   I ain't losin my rag, awright.

Gina   OK.

Barry   Stop sayin OK. I'm juss sayin, I'm tellin yer, I'm not my brother. I want to watch the match. Wat Mark does is up to him. I don't want to be like 'em. Go all mad all the time, I don't.

Lee *comes in followed by* **Lawrie** *and* **Alan**.

Lawrie   You soft cunt. I'm talkin to you.

Becks   Wat?

Lawrie   He only tells his mates to let that Sharon off.

Lee   I didn't see the point in taking it through.

Alan   The point was made when they put the cuffs on her.

Lawrie   She only bit one of them.

Alan   You can't change people like that.

Lee   And you juss had to stand there, stirring it.

Lawrie   Lee, she went for yer, she coulda had a knife.

Lee   You see knives everywhere, Lawrie. Whenever we go out, whenever you see a black person, you think they've got a knife.

Lawrie   Well, pardon me for caring.

Lee   I'm awright.

Lawrie Ungrateful or wat, eh?

Alan Comfortable is it? The fence you're sitting on?

Lee Get out of my face.

Lawrie Oh, leave him. I don't know wass the matter wid him.

Alan Don't ever lose your rag like that again.

Lawrie Eh?

Alan You were this much from getting arrested as well. Is it any wonder no one listens to us?

Lawrie Hold up.

Alan I couldn't believe my eyes when I saw you lot running amok in Belgium. What was that?

Lawrie It's about bein English. All the things you've said.

Alan That wasn't bein English, you were acting like a bunch of savages.

Lawrie It's how I feel.

Alan That's no excuse.

Lawrie There's nuttin that makes me wanna say I'm proud to be English.

Alan No one wants to speak up for you. It's not fashionable.

Lawrie Right.

Alan But they want to speak up for the blacks, queers, Pakis, that's fashionable.

Lawrie Yes!

Alan You just want to run out and beat the shit out of someone.

Lawrie So wass the problem?

Alan It scares people.

Lawrie It don't scare me.

Alan   You don't speak for the country.

Lawrie   So, what?

Alan   It's the smart arses who are in control of this country, on every level, and we have to be as clever. Keep this country white, away from the blacks. They're just marginalising them. Don't let them marginalise us. Gina's right, get your head out of rubbish like the *Sun*, get down the library, read a book, read ten books.

Lawrie   I hate books.

Alan   Not any more. I'll give you a list. Because knowledge is power.

Lawrie (*scoffs*)   Come on, Alan.

Alan   Read.

They continue their game of pool. **Lee** *is by the bar with* **Gina**. *The lads are still watching the game.*

Jason   We should be wearing our home kit. The blue and white.

Becks   Why?

Jason   We always seem to play worse in our red. Wat do you think?

Phil   I think yer talkin shit.

Jason   Look.

Phil   We wore red in '66, and won.

Becks   We wore white and blue in the semis in Italy and lost.

Barry   We wore all white against the Argies in '98 and lost.

Phil   And in Euro '96, against the fuckin Germans again!

Barry   No we didn't.

Phil   We did lose.

Barry   I mean we wore all blue for that, yer muppet.

Phil   Oh, right. I musta bin thinkin about the other game.

Jason   I hated that blue kit.

Becks   Everyone hated it.

Barry   Our home kit then was awright, I like that. I don't know why they changed it. I really liked the touch of light blue it had, on the collars and cuff, and that bit on the shorts.

Boys (*agreeing*)   Yeah.

Barry   Nice.

Phil   I thought the last one we had was awright as well, with the blue and the red stripes down the sides. With a touch of white on the blue shorts.

Boys (*agreeing*)   Yeah.

Phil   Very nice.

Gina   I don't care what colour she is. She deserves to be carted off. Mouthin off like that.

Lee   Lawrie didn't help. I'm so sick of this. He won't listen.

Gina   He loves his football.

Lee   From the day he was born. Thirtieth July '66.

Gina   And?

Lee   Day England won the World Cup.

Gina   Shut up.

Lee   On my life.

Gina   No way!

Lee   Dad wanted to name him after Geoff Hurst.

Gina *laughs.*

Lee   Mum wouldn't have it. You know how many times I've heard Dad going on about that match, describing every goal? When England ruled the world again for four glorious years, when Enoch spoke the truth. Lawrie loved that shit.

Gina   Wait till I tell Dad.

Lee   I can't do it, Gina.

Gina   Do wat?

Lee   The job. He's my brother, he gets on my tits, but I feel like agreeing with him sometimes. Cos thass the bitta Dad rubbing off on me. But that's not the kind of copper I want to be. But then I'm thinkin it's too late. Whenever a black geezer comes up to me now, I'm shakin. All I wanted to do that night, Gina, was calm it all down. All the things they moan about on the tele, all the things police officers don't do, that they hate, what they should be doing, well I was doing it! All of it! I was treating all those people at that rave, like people, not black people, but people! I wanted to understand, I was trying to listen, I wanted to prove that not all coppers are the same. Then he stabbed me. That fuckin black bastard stabbed me. I ain't racist, Gina, but it's how I feel, is that so wrong? That bloke tried to kill me, and he got away with it.

Gina   I ain't judging yer.

Lee   All I wanted to do was help.

Gina   There's yer problem. Don't help them. Don't try to understand them. Do yer job. Don't lose yerself, Lee.

Phil   Oh come on!

Jason   Fuck's sake

Becks   They're gettin comfortable again, we gotta keep possession, gotta push 'em back, see how they like it in their own half for once.

Jason   Oh, you useless wankers, come on. Please! I'm beggin yer!

The boys get excited as Le Saux makes a run.

Yes, yes!

Phil   Come on, Le Saux!

Becks   Come on, Le Saux!

Jason   Fuckin cross it!

The German defender heads it away.

Phil   Shit.

Jason   Wass he head that away for? Let us have one, yer greedy cunts!

Barry *leaves his seat.*

Jason   Where you goin, Baz? Baz? (*Mimics* **Barry**.) All I'm doing is watchin the match.

Barry *goes to the pool table.*

Alan   How are we doing?

Barry   My name was on the board.

Alan   Was it?

Barry   I was supposed to be playing next.

Lawrie   Yeah?

Alan   Lawrie?

Lawrie *steps aside as* **Barry** *picks up a cue.*

Alan   We are all friends here.

Barry *and* **Alan** *play pool together.* **Lawrie** *watches on.*

Alan   So, how is it going?

Barry   Awright.

Alan   That was a splendid couple of goals you got this morning. Did you ever think about turning pro?

Barry   Had a trial for Fulham. Didn't cut it.

Alan   Their loss. Who do you follow?

Barry   Man U.

Alan   Man U?

Barry   Ain't they good enough?

Alan   Comedian.

Lawrie I'd shit on Man U.

Alan Yes, that is very nice, Lawrie, but no one is asking you, are they? (*To* **Barry**.) Follow your local team, what is the matter with you? It's about loyalty. Family even. You don't choose your family, they are just there, from the moment you are born. Through thick and thin. There with you, you're with them. You are born in the town of your team. They are your family as well, your blood. And every Saturday, you are watching them play, willing them on to score, then another, and another.

Barry Final whistle goes.

Alan And you all roar and cheer.

Barry You can't wait till next Saturday.

Alan Starts all over again.

Barry I love that feeling.

Alan And no matter where you go, where you move. You take them with you, in your heart.

Barry I know.

Alan When was the last time you've been to Old Trafford?

Barry Does it matter? I follow them.

Alan But do you feel them?

Barry Course.

Alan Where were you born?

Barry Shepherds Bush.

Alan Queens Park Rangers.

Barry They're shit.

Alan They're yer blood.

Barry I ain't following them.

Alan Just as you like.

Barry So who do you follow?

Alan   Aston Villa. What are you laughing at? My dad
followed Villa. I was born in Birmingham. We all moved to
London when I was ten. But I took them with me, in my heart.

Barry   You still watch them?

Alan   Whenever I can. I can still remember my first game.
My dad took me when I was nine. 1961 it was. We beat
Sheffield Wednesday 4–1. We played them off the park. And
it was Johnny Dixon's last game for Villa.

Barry   Who?

Alan   One of the best forwards we ever had. He stayed with
the club for seventeen years. He could score goals as well as
make them. He was our captain when we won the cup in '57.
What a game. I've still got the programme. Still, Man U are a
blinding side, can't argue with that. Your Andy Cole is doing
all right for himself, and the other one, wasshisface.

Barry   Dwight Yorke. Used to be one of yours.

Alan   Yes, all right, don't rub it in. Class player he was.

Barry   Still is.

Alan   Always smiling. Should have seen the verbal he got
from some of the fans though when he came back to Villa,
wearing a Man U shirt. Black this, black that! I have never
heard anything like it. What was it that them Liverpool fans
used to chant at John Barnes when he first started playing for
them? Lawrie?

Lawrie   Better dead, than a nigger in red.

Alan   Right. Must be hard for you as well.

Barry   I never get it.

Alan   Well, then you are lucky. Isn't he lucky, Lawrie?

Lawrie   Yeah, he's lucky.

Alan   It's good to hear that. It gives hope to us all. You are a
black person who everyone sees as a person first, not their
colour.

Barry   I am a person.

Alan   That is what I said. Never mind the ones who only see you as a black person. Have you ever ran into those people, son?

Barry   No.

Alan   The ones who think being white is the norm?

Barry   I said no.

Alan   Awright, son. I'm just trying to put myself in your shoes. No need to get jumpy.

Barry   I'm not jumpy.

Alan   I understand where you are coming from, I really do. You're from this country, you live here, born here, but there are still a few, the minority, that won't accept you,

Barry   I am accepted.

Alan   Course you are. I mean, you're not like the Asians, are you?

Barry   Too right.

Alan   No. I don't see your lot owning hundreds of shops all lined up next to each other down Southall. Cutting yourselves off from the rest of the country. Not speaking the Queen's English. Your lot ain't like that at all. You're sweet with us now. It must get to you though, when you meet the ones who just want to know about the black experience.

Barry   That ain't me.

Alan   White girls, eyeing you up all the time, because they're curious about the myth, do you all have third legs? White guys wanting to be your mates, because they are curious as well. Penis-envy, hardly acceptance, is it, Barry?

Barry   Wass the matter wid yer?

Alan   Then there's the bleeding-heart liberals, lining up, wanting to do you all a favour, they just want to tick their boxes, they're scared you'll lose your tempers, mug them after work, how equal is that? All that talk, understanding, deep down they know, they believe, blacks are inferior, whites are superior. You must feel really small when you meet people like that . . .

Barry   . . . Look, juss fuck off, awright!

He rejoins the others.

Alan   Barry? Barry son?

Lawrie   Wat was that?

Alan   Reeling them in, throwing them back. The boy's got no idea who his friends are.

Phil   Oh look, he's bringin a sub on.

Becks   Oh nice one, Keegan, yer muppet!

Barry (*screams*)   Come on, you England!

Jason   Baz?

Barry   Stand up if you won the war! Stand up if you won the war!

Jason   Not again.

Barry   You dirty German bastard! You dirty German bastard!

Jason   Barry!

Barry   ENGLAND!

Jimmy   Oi, Lionel Ritchie, keep it down, yeah?

Mark *comes back into the pub.*

Jimmy   You going to be nice now?

Mark   Leave me alone, Jimmy.

Jimmy   I can't do that. Leave the attitude outside, Mark.

Mark   I'm juss watching the game.

Jimmy   Wat happened to that happy little smilin coloured kid I used to know, eh? Good little boy? Go on, sit down.

Mark *joins the boys, sits near* **Lee**.

Jason   Wat do you call that?

Lee   You go to the station?

Mark   They had to drag her in there.

Lee   She was resisting arrest, Mark.

Mark   Like an animal.

Lee   Wat were they supposed to do?

Mark   Four coppers, one woman.

Lee   You saw how she was.

Mark   Four coppers, one woman.

Lee   You never listen, it's your point of view or nuttin.

Jimmy   Mark?

Lee   We're all right, Jimmy. (*To* **Mark**.) I tried to calm the situation as well as I could.

Mark   You takin the piss?

Lee *goes to the bar.*

Mark   Wat you runnin for?

Lee   Top it up, Gina.

Mark   Wat you runnin for?

Gina   Leave it out, Mark.

Mark   You really think she deserved to be treated like that?

Lee   Why you always pushin me?

Mark   Do yer, Lee?

Gina   He was doing his job.

Mark   Stick together, like old times ennit?

Gina   Oh piss off!

Lee   Bloody . . .

Mark   Say it, Lee, call me a nigger again.

Lee   He really wants me to.

Mark   It's wat I am!

Gina   Will you stop!

Mark   You didn't want me havin her cos I was black.

Gina   Oh Mark.

Lee   White guy steals white girl from black guy, it juss doesn't happen, does it, Mark? It's the other way round.

Mark   You wanted to finish wid me cos I was black.

Gina   I finished wid you cos you were boring. You were boring in bed, and you were boring to talk to. If you woke up tomorrow, as white as I am, you'll still be boring.

Jimmy (*approaches*)   I warned you, son, come on.

Gina   Leave it alone, Dad.

Barry   ENGER-LAND! ENGER-LAND! ENGER-LAND!

Becks   Awright, Baz, Jesus!

Gina   Will you sort him out please?

Mark (*approaches*)   Barry, come on.

Barry   Wass up, bro? My brother! He's more English than any of you, he's protected this country. He's protected you! Come on, you England! Stand up if you won the war!

Gina   Take him home.

Barry   Game ain't finished.

Mark   He'll be awright. Come on!

Becks   Wat, again? They tugging each other's plonkers or wat?

Jimmy   Wass wrong with that boy?

Lights on **Barry** *and* **Mark** *in the Gents.*

Barry   Fucking bastard! 'Bout I ain't English.

Mark   Who?

Barry   That geezer Alan. Talkin to me like I'm stupid.

Mark   You shoulda stayed away from him.

Barry   Shoulda told him about Euro '96. Wembley, Holland, the game!

Mark   I know.

Barry   We killed them, oh man we killed them! Four goals, class written all over them. The best match since '66. Saw it wid me own eyes. You, me and Lee. Cheering the lads on, singing our hearts out. I backed you and Lee up when those bunch of Dutch fans tried to have a pop, we kicked every bit of shit out of them. Then we roared, right into their faces, England! Shoulda told him that, then give him a fuckin slap. He was all nice to me as well.

Mark   They only pretend to be yer friends.

Barry   I don't have problems with the rest of them.

Mark   Not yet.

Barry   What are we, a couple of Pakis now? Wass happened to you?

Mark   I juss saw Sharon dragged by her hair.

Barry   Sharon's a bitch.

Mark   So, she deserve that?

Barry   Stop using her as an excuse.

Mark   I ain't.

Barry   You are.

Mark   Look, yer right, I don't want to go home either. I don't want to see Dad like that. So let's get out of here, check out Daryl and dem, I bet they're watchin the match.

Barry I don't like Daryl and his mates.

Mark You shouldn't be afraid of yer own people.

Barry I ain't afraid of them, I juss don't like some of 'em. You feel the same, Mark, well, used to. I loved the way you were with them. Them carryin on with their bad attitude, you used to slap them down, they were havin a laugh. Wass the army done to you? (*Takes off his shirt, shows his tattoo.*) Look.

Mark Barry . . .

Barry Thass British, thass us! Don't laugh at me, it's us. Show me yours.

Mark Get off.

Barry You were gonna wear it wid pride, you said. You didn't care who sees your red, white and blue, or who laughs, cos you ain't ending up like some black cunt. We are British, we are here! We kick arse with the best of them. God save the Queen, you told me that.

Mark They don't want us here, Barry.

Barry We were born here.

Mark They don't care.

Lights up on the bar.

Glen *comes down. The screen turns blue again. Lads groan.*

Becks Oh shut up, yer gettin on my tits now, the lot of yer.

Gina How's my little prince, then?

Glen Awright.

Gina Yer still gorgeous. (*Kisses him on the cheek.*)

Glen (*embarrassed*) Mum?

Jimmy You stopped cryin, then?

Gina Dad? I thought you were going to watch telly?

Glen Nuttin's on.

Gina   Watch a video, then. (*Gets a fiver from the till.*) Here, go down the video shop.

Glen   I don't want to go out.

Gina   You can't stay in here for ever, sweetheart. You're going to have to face those boys again.

Glen   I know I have to face them again, Mum, but I don't want to do it now.

Gina   Calm down, I'm on your side, darlin. Go on, sit with the lads, watch the game. Go on, they don't bite.

Glen *joins* **Lee** *and the others. They all greet him warmly.*

Jason   Awright, Glen?

Phil   How you doing, son?

Lawrie   You want a Coke, Glen?

Glen   Yeah.

Gina   Yeah wat?

Glen   Yeah please.

Gina   Cheers, Lawrie.

Lawrie   Top this up as well, Gina.

Jason   Come on, Glen, cheer up.

Becks   Wat goes around, comes around.

Phil   This whole area is going down.

Becks   See Glen, wat you have to do, is get a little gang of yer own, you and a few white lads.

Jason   Don't let Gina hear yer.

Lee   Or me!

Becks   There's nuttin wrong wid that?

Lee   You sure?

Becks   I've seen black gangs, Asian gangs, how can it be racist if them boys are doing it? Get yerself some white boys

Glen, stick together, show some pride. (*To screen.*) Unlike these wankers!

Lee (*to* **Glen**)   Oi, you ignore every word he said, you hear me?

Phil   Glen, come here, got a joke for yer. There's this black geezer right, Winston, nice fella, well thick. Anyway, he's feelin a sick one morning, so he rings up his boss at work sayin – (*Puts on a bad West Indian accent.*) 'Ey, boss, I not come work today, I really sick. I got headache, stomach ache, and my legs hurt, I not come work.' The boss goes, 'Oh Winston, you know I really need you today. It's important. Now, when I feel like this, I go to my wife, and tell her to give me sex. That makes me feel better and I can go to work. You should try that.' Two hours later, Winston calls back, saying, 'Boss, boss, I did wat you said and I feel great, man! I be back at work real soon, boss. By the way, you got a nice house!'

The boys roar with laughter.

Phil   Oops, I can see a smile, a smile is coming, he's smiling, he's smiling!

Boys cheer.

Lee   Is anyone watchin the match here?

Phil   What match?

Jason   Useless cunts.

Phil   Ere, Glen, come here. Yer mum still got that same boyfriend?

Glen   No. Why?

Phil   Nuttin.

Barry *and* **Mark** *come back*

Becks   Barry, my man, where you bin?

Jason   Have a nice tug, did yer? (*Rubs* **Barry**'s *head.*)

Barry   Don't.

Jason   Oooh, handbag.

Gina   We happy over there?

Mark   Sweet as, Gina.

Alan   Fancy a game, son?

Mark   I'm outta here.

Alan   Come on, one game.

Mark   Play me like you did my brother?

Alan   I'm sorry?

Mark   Don't even try.

Alan   All right, then. But I bet you've fantasised about having a debate with someone like me.

Mark   I've fantasised about kicking the shit out of someone like you.

Alan   That would be too easy.

Mark   We got nuttin in common.

Alan   Let's see. (*Offers a cue-stick.*) Do you know what the main thing is that I hear people moan about? It's that they don't think they can talk about it. They can't voice their concerns, how they feel, they're too scared to be called racists by the PC brigade. Now, I don't know about you, Mark, but I think we've got to get through that, because if people can't talk to each other, we are not going to get anywhere. So, come on. You and me, let's pave the way. If you want to stop people from being like me, then you had better start listening to people like me.

Mark *takes the cue-stick.*

Alan   So, army boy.

Mark   Ex.

Alan   What happened?

Mark   My CO was a racist wanker, so I smacked him one.

Alan   Nasty.

Mark   For him.

Alan   Do you know what you are going to do now?

Mark   You gonna give me a job? Let's get on with it.

Alan   Putting me straight. I like that. Do you watch TV, Mark?

Mark (*sarcastic*)   Once or twice.

Alan   All of those chat shows they have in the morning. *Trisha, Kilroy*, Richard and Judy –

Mark   Is there a point coming?

Alan   Any time they have some big issue to bang on about, they invite the general public, the great working class, to have their say. Live debates, phone-ins, big mistake. I shudder when I hear them speak. Cringe. They are so inarticulate, they cannot string two sentences together. And their arguments, their points of view, Jesus Christ! It's obvious they have never read a book in their lives. I've seen black people on those programmes as well, son, and no offence, but it seems as though they've eaten retard sandwiches. Have you ever felt that way about them?

Mark   No.

Alan   Come on, Mark, honesty. Play the game.

Mark   Yes.

Alan   You hate the way they talk.

Mark   Yes.

Alan   They're letting the side down.

Mark   Yes.

Alan   Make your point, and make it well.

Mark   You gonna make yours?

Alan   You want to be better than that, but that can never happen. Not here.

Mark   Wat?

Alan   Look at us, Mark. (*Points at everyone.*) The white working class. You think it was an accident we are all as thick as shit? Britain needs people like Lawrie to do the crap jobs. It can't have everyone bein a doctor or a lawyer, the economy would fall apart, and do you know who we're are going to blame for not getting ahead? You. Why? Because you're different, because it's convenient, because it's easier to blame you than it is to think about what's really going on, and the reason why we don't think is because we can't, and the reason we can't is because the ones in power made sure of it. Spin us a tale, put it in the tabloids, we'll buy it. We'll blame anyone that is different for our own shortcomings. They want us to fight, they want us to fight you. We'll fight, but not they way they think. This is our country, we made it, and we don't belong in the gutter because they say we do.

Mark   But we do?

Alan   I didn't say that.

Mark   Gimme one good reason why I shouldn't wrap this cue-stick round yer head.

Alan   Because I can help you.

Mark   By sending me back to where I come from?

Alan   We don't believe in that any more.

Mark *sneers.*

Alan   You're not our enemy, son.

Mark   Don't call me son.

Alan   Our fight is with the government and their soppy immigration laws that keeps throwing us all together. It's not working, is it? Why don't you work with us?

Mark   What?

Alan   Spend some time with us? It's not as uncommon as you think. Some of our European friends have had black and Jewish branches. We're thinking of setting up our own ethnic liaison committee.

Mark   Yer certifiable.

Alan   Don't tell me you're happy wid the way yer lot carry on, especially round here.

Mark   I know how I feel, and yeah, they make me sick to be black. All they're doin is provin you and me right. But I don't want to be right any more, I want to be proved wrong. I'm sick of being angry.

Alan   That's soppy talk.

Mark   I want to be who I want.

Alan   So be it, but don't wait for this government. You have to make your own mark in this world, son, no one else will do it for you.

Mark (*laughs*)   You sound like my dad.

Alan   Wise man, was he?

Mark   He thought he was.

Alan   What did he do?

Mark   Bus conductor.

Alan   How long?

Mark   Thirty-odd years.

Alan   And I bet he had to scrimp and save all his life.

Mark   Who doesn't?

Alan   But that is not what he wanted when he came here, I bet. Or are you telling me he left the sun and sea of the West Indies for the grey skies of London to be a bus conductor? The poor sod probably wanted to party all night, sleep with as many women as possible, and smoke loads of shit.

Mark *bursts out laughing*

Alan   You looked at him, and you thought, no way am I ending up like that. But you are, it's still happening. No one is going to help you.

Mark   I don't want help.

Alan   You all want it, you're lost without it.

Mark   I want a chance.

Alan   But it is white people in power that's pulling all the strings, Mark. They'll decide how many chances you get. They're always going to be above you, that's never going to change, so stop wishing. Show me one white person who has ever treated you as an equal, and I will show you a liar. All this multiculturalism. Eating a mango once a year at the Notting Hill Carnival is still a long way from letting your kids go to a school that is overrun with Pakis and blacks.

Mark   I'm English.

Alan   No you're not.

Mark   I served in Northern Ireland.

Alan   Oh, please.

Mark   How English are you? Where do you draw the line as to who's English? I was born in this country. And my brother. You're white, your culture comes from Northern Europe, Scandinavia, Denmark. Your people moved from there thousands of years ago, what? You think cos I'm black, I don't read books. Where do you draw the line?

Alan   That is such a ridiculous question.

Mark   Answer me.

Alan   The fact is, Mark, that the white British are a majority racial group in this country, therefore it belongs to the white British. If that was the case, what you're asking, we'd all be putting ourselves back into the sea. Because that is where we all originally came from, isn't it?

Mark   Yer full of shit.

Alan   We say that the people of European, white European descent are entitled to settle in Britain. Or the rest of Europe, where they are. We regard our racial cousins, the Americans,

Canadians, as British. They've been implanted there over the centuries, now why should we take a time on it? The fact is the majority of blacks haven't been in this country for centuries, a few yes, maybe, but that's it. You've been here, predominantly, in your own numbers, three generations at most. That gives you squatters' rights. You have given nothing to Britain, and you have never served any purpose in British history.

Mark   Oh, so the fact that thousands of black soldiers died during the war is lost on you?

Alan   Oh, don't waste my time.

Mark   Or the fact that in the eighteenth century there was a thriving black community, living right here?

Alan   Not as many as the Brits.

Mark   With their own pubs, churches, meeting places. Or the fact that in 1596 there were so many black slaves over here, working for their white owners, putting money in their pockets, doing all the work, that Queen Elizabeth saw them as a threat and wanted them out.

Alan   What are you on?

Mark   How many black Roman soldiers were here, when they came over and built your roads?

Alan   You're losing it.

Mark   Were you bullied at school, Alan? Couple of black kids nicked your dinner money? Or did your wife run off with a big black man? And I mean big black man? Or was it your mum?

Alan   If you're so smart, son, how come you still haven't caught up with us?

Mark   Cos you love pushing us down.

Alan   Well, push us back. You've had thousands of years. What are you waiting for? Always some excuse. Can't you people take account for what you are doing to yourselves, instead of blaming us every five seconds?

Mark   You are to blame.

Alan   If you cannot hold your own to account for what they are doing, then we will be left to take drastic measures.

Mark   Is that right?

Alan   Lack of accountability creates anger, Mark, look at all the hate in the world, and it will twist some people's logic, just like Lawrie's, and flavour thought. Bad things are motivated purely by anger. You lot need to feel we will be held to account for what we've done, well,we need to feel it from you first.

Mark   You don't have the right.

Alan   Why's that?

Mark   Because yer white.

Alan   Who's the bigot now?

Mark   Go fuck yourself.

Alan   Face it, son, you are nothing but a ticked box.

Mark   You won't win.

Alan   We already have.

Mark (*chants*)   We shall not, we shall not be moved!

Alan   Mark?

Mark   We shall not, we shall not be moved, we shall not, we shall not be moved, we shall not, we shall not be moved, we shall not, we shall not be moved! We shall not, we shall not be moved, we shall not, we shall not be moved, we shall not, we shall not be moved . . . Baz!

Barry (*joins in*)   We shall not, we shall not be moved! We shall not, we shall not be moved . . .

Mark/Barry   We shall not, we shall not be moved! We shall not, we shall not be moved, and we'll go on, to win the great World Cup, we shall not be moved!

Phil   You two pissed?

Mark/Barry ENGLAND! (*Clap.*) ENGLAND! (*Clap.*)
ENGLAND! (*Clap.*) ENGLAND! (*Clap.*) ENGLAND!

Lawrie (*approaches*)   You awright, Alan?

Alan   They can't even see when someone is doing them a
favour. I've got half a mind to set you on him.

Lawrie   Why don't yer?

Alan   Don't be stupid.

Lawrie   I'll be careful.

Lee *comes out of the Gents.*

Lawrie   Say the word and he's dead.

Lee   Who's dead?

Alan   We are.

Lee   Who's dead, Lawrie?

Lawrie   No one.

Lee (*to* **Alan**)   You, fuck off.

Alan   I beg your pardon?

Lee   I'm talking to my brother.

Alan (*approaches*)   Another scotch, Gina.

Lee   You touch Mark, I'll have yer.

Lawrie   Easy, boy.

Lee   I've had enuff of yer shit, Lawrie.

Lawrie   Why are you still sticking up for them?

Lee   It weren't Mark that stabbed me.

Lawrie   They're scum.

Lee   I won't let you.

Lawrie   Who held yer hand every night while you had yer
nightmares, Lee? Do you still see him when you shut yer eyes?
That coon coming at yer with his knife?

Lee   It's me he tried to kill.

Lawrie   And I want to kill every one of them.

Lee   Yer never happy unless yer gettin stuck in on someone's head.

Lawrie   Go on, fuck off, go back to yer posh bird.

Lee   If you weren't such a prick, you'd come live with us.

Lawrie   I ain't no ponce.

Lee   You need looking after.

Lawrie   Yer my little brother, you don't look after me. God, I feel like I want to explode sometimes.

Lee   See.

Lawrie   I woulda killed someone by now if it weren't for Alan. I really would. I can feel myself wantin to do it sometimes. Every morning when I wake up. I wanna make a bomb or summin, go down Brixton and blow every one of them up.

Lee   Do you want me to choose, Lawrie?

Lawrie   Do wat you want.

Lee   I want me brother.

Lawrie   I'm here.

Lee   Ask Alan about Reading, watch his face drop.

Lawrie   Wat about it?

Lee   I've been checking on him. Him and his lot were recruiting teenagers. One of them got a little excited, beat up some Asian kid. Alan, blindin geezer, didn't even wait for the old bill to breath down his neck. He gave up that boy's name so fast, well desperate to save his arse. You want that to be you?

Lawrie   That kid was stupid, he got caught.

Lee   Why won't you ever listen to me?

Lawrie   I ain't you, Lee.

Lee   Fucking Dad.

Lawrie (*snaps*)   Don't!

Lee   Don't think I won't warn him.

Lawrie   You think thass gonna stop me?

The final whistle blows. The game is finished.

Jason   Wat a load of fuckin bollocks.

Screen shows Kevin Keegan walking away with his head down. Sound of the crowd booing.

Yeah, nice one, lads, boo the cunt!

The boys join in the jeering.

Jimmy   Southgate in midfield!

Phil   Cole up front wid Owen!

Becks   Lass game at Wembley!

Phil   You see that? Hamman's wearing an England sweater.

Barry   Who swapped jerseys?

Phil   It's a number four he's wearin.

Becks   Southgate.

Barry   Fuckin Kraut-lover. We lose one–nil and he's given him his jersey.

Becks's *phone rings.*

Becks (*answers*)   Awright, Rob? Yeah I know, fuckin disgrace ennit? Wat? Rob goes the fans are booing Keegan.

Jason   They wanna fuckin lynch him.

Mark   Come on, who's drinkin?

Phil   Yeah, go on then, with any luck I might drown the memory of this day away.

Barry   Lass game at Wembley.

Mark   They're buildin a new one.

Barry   Won't be the same.

Becks   Awright, see yer in a bit. (*Hangs up.*) Rob's gonna come over. Well, come on, lets have some beer.

Jason   Yeah, whose round is it, Becks?

Mark   Na, yer awright, I'll get 'em in.

Becks   Cheers, Mark.

Mark   Barry?

Barry *goes with his brother.*

Jason   You are so bleeding tight, Becks. You ain't put yer hand in yer pocket all day, have yer?

Becks   Is it my fault our coloured friends over there are so generous? Come on, smile, yer cunts. We can still get to the finals, it's not impossible. We'll beat the Germans next year.

Phil   Oh yeah, we're really gonna hammer them on their own turf, ain't we?

Jason   Wat do you reckon the score will be, Becks, five–one to us?

Becks   Sod yer then.

Lee *approaches* **Barry** *and* **Mark**.

Lee   You gotta get out of here. Both of yer.

Mark   Why's that?

Lee   Lawrie's on the warpath, I don't know if I can hold him back.

Mark   You've never tried

Lee   Come on, not now.

Barry   He's gonna have a pop in front of everyone?

Lee   He doesn't care. Look, juss go, awright.

Barry   Mark?

Mark   We're stayin.

Lee   He's gonna do some damage.

Mark   It's nice to know you care.

Lee   Yer my best mate

Mark   Were.

Lee   Are!

Mark   Then why'd you say it, Lee?

Lee   I'm sorry, fer fuck's sake.

Mark   If that walrus wants to have a pop, let 'im.

A brick comes smashing through one of the windows.

Phil   Oh fuck!

Jason   Jesus!

Gina   Dad!

Phil   I'm cut.

Jimmy (*sees the window*)   Christ.

Phil   Bastards!

Gina   You awright, Phil?

Phil   Do I look it?

Gina   Glen, get me the first-aid box.

Alan (*peers out of the window*)   You had better get the police as well. There is a whole army of black kids out there.

Jason (*looks out*)   Jesus!

Another brick comes flying through.

Jason   Oi! You black cunt.

Lee   Shut up, Jase.

Jason They're lobbing bricks at us, wat you want?

Lee I'm going out there.

Lawrie (*concerned*) Lee?

Lee You stay.

Alan Lawrence. (*To* **Lee**.) He'll be all right.

Mark Lee, hold up, mate.

Lee Jimmy, call the police.

Gina Tell them if they step one foot in my pub, there'll be murders.

Mark *and* **Lee** *go out.* **Gina** *treats* **Phil**'s *wounds from the first-aid box.*

Becks (*looks through the window*) Thass the little sod who took Glen's phone.

Glen *runs behind the bar and goes upstairs.*

Gina Glen, come back here! Glen!

Phil He'll be awright. He's a good kid.

Gina Oi, stop lookin at my tits.

Phil I can't help it. They're lovely.

Gina Excuse me?

Phil Yer lovely.

Gina Am I now?

Phil Yeah.

Gina You don't half pick yer moments, Philip.

Jimmy *approaches holding* **Glen** *by his ear.*

Jimmy He was only trying to sneak out through the back door.

Gina Wat you playing at?

Glen   It's my problem, right, I'm gonna deal wid dem.

Jimmy   Listen to him. The boy's got sum bottle after all.

Glen   Ennit!

Jimmy   Shame about his brain. There's a whole bleedin tribe out there, you wanna take them on?

Gina   You wanna do summin? Go change the loo rolls in the Gents.

Glen *goes to do as he is told.*

Gina   You call the police?

Jimmy   They're comin.

Becks   Might not need 'em now. Lee is doing the business, tellin them to back off. (*To* **Barry**.) And yer Mark. They make a good team.

Phil   Send one of them bastards in here, I'll do the business on them.

Gina (*shouts by door*)   Mark? Lee? You find the bastards who broke my winder and tell them they owe me money.

Some of the crowd shout obscenities at **Gina**.

Gina   Yeah, fuck you an all. (*Shuts the door.*)

Mark *and* **Lee** *come back in.*

Barry   You awright, bruv?

Mark   Yeah. Thanks ever so much for helpin out there, Gina, very useful.

Gina   I weren't jokin, Mark, I want money for my winders.

Mark   It coulda bin worse.

Lee   They were well pissed.

Mark   Speakin of which.

He goes into the Gents.

Lee   I don't know how long me and Mark held them off for, they could come back. You call the police?

Jimmy   On way.

Lee *catches sight of* **Lawrie**, *who looks like he's heading for the Gents.*

Lee   Lawrie? Lawrie!

Lawrie *in fact detours slightly and goes to the cigarette machine, where he buys a packet of fags.*

Lawrie (*as calm as you like*)   Wat?

He walks back to the pool table.

On the screen, Keegan is being interviewed.

Jimmy   Wass he goin on about, Jase?

Jason   He's only fuckin quit.

Phil   Wat?

Jason   Straight up, Keegan's quit!

Phil   Muppet.

Jimmy   Jesus.

Becks   Well, I won't miss him, dozey sod . . .

Lawrie *throws the cue across the pool table.*

Gina   Lawrie!

Jimmy   If yer old man was still alive, he'd tan yer arse.

Lawrie   Keegan's got no backbone, Jimmy, this whole country's lost its spine.

Jimmy   Oh, piss off

Lawrie   We ruled the world.

Lee (*approaches*)   Broth.

Lawrie   Go play wid yer monkey friends.

Becks   Ease up, Lawrie.

Lawrie   Did I ask yer for anything?

Becks (*scared*)   Nuh, mate, you didn't.

Lawrie *catches* **Barry***'s eye.*

Lawrie   You wanna have a pop? Well, come on then, black boy, show us how English you are.

Lee   Back off, Barry.

Barry   He challenged me.

Lee   He'll kill yer.

Lawrie   I'll have you, then those monkeys out there.

Gina *gets her baseball bat from behind the bar and waves it around.*

Becks   Whoa!

Gina   Not in my pub, you understand? Be told.

Jason   Yeah, Gina,watever you say.

Phil   I'm told.

Alan   Lawrie? (*Motions him to come over.*) Here!

Lee   Don't.

Gina   Leave him alone, Lee. He's a big boy.

Lawrie (*approaches*)   Why didn't you say anything?

Alan   Why won't you listen?

Lawrie   Cos I can't. Awright!

Alan   You won't even give yourself a chance. The smart-arses want to write you off as a brainless wanker, and you're letting them.

Lawrie   Juss let me have 'em. I won't mess up, I ain't stupid like that kid in Reading.

Alan   What do you know about Reading?

Lawrie   Got it from Lee. If this kid got himself caught, then thass his lookout.

Alan   The kid's name was Brian.

Lawrie   You gonna let me?

Alan   You remind me of him. Short fuse, kept running off on his own.

Lawrie   Come on, Alan.

Alan   I had enough. He wouldn't listen. And I don't have time for people who refuse to listen.

Lawrie   Well, I'm tired of waiting. I wanted him. He wanted me. They all want it. Ask any coon. Let's juss stop all this fuckin about and get it on. Lass one standing at the final whistle wins England.

Alan   You gotta trust me, my way is the only way forward.

Lawrie   No wonder this Brian kid got pissed off with yer. I mean fer fuck's sake, Alan, d'yer really think those smart-arses are gonna let us be as clever as them? I don't even want it.

Glen *is changing the loo paper in the Gents.* **Mark** *comes out of the next cubicle.*

Mark   You awright?

Glen *is getting frustrated as he cannot seem to get the finished loo roll off.*

Mark   Let me help.

Glen   No.

Mark   Don't be silly, there's nuttin to it.

Glen   Move.

He shoves him, and as he does a long kitchen knife drops from inside his jacket onto the floor. He picks it quickly, but **Mark** *has already seen it.*

Mark   Wat you doin wid that? Do you want me to go out and get yer mum, wat you doin wid that?

Glen   They fuck wid me, I'm gonna fuck wid them.

Mark   No, no, that ain't the way, Glen.

Glen   You lot, you think yer so fuckin bad, I'll show you
who's bad.

Mark   But this ain't the way. Duane and Tyrone, yeah,
they're juss boys. Not black boys, but juss boys. Stupid boys.

Glen   They're on us every day at school, all the white kids.
Cos they think they're bad.

Mark   They're stupid boys, Glen.

Glen   You gonna move.

Mark   We are not all the same.

Glen   Move.

Mark   Juss gimme the knife.

He moves to disarm him. **Glen** *dodges* **Mark** *and stabs him in the
stomach.* **Mark** *drops to the floor.* **Glen** *cannot quite take in what he
has done. He dashes out. Goes upstairs.*

Gina   You finished? Glen? Fine, ignore me why don't yer.

Lawrie *pops to the Gents. He sees* **Mark***'s bleeding body and comes
rushing out.*

Lawrie   We gotta go.

Alan   I don't waste my time on losers, Lawrie, piss off.

Lawrie   Alan! We gotta go.

Alan   What have you done?

Lawrie   Nothing

Jason *(comes running out of the Gents)*   Oh shit!

Gina   Wat?

Jason   It's Mark?

Barry   Bruv? *(Sees* **Mark***.)* Mark!

Lee   Don't touch him.

Barry   Get off me.

Lee   Let me see, let me see.

Barry   Ambulance!

Lee   Barry, listen.

Barry   Get off me.

Gina   Christ!

Lee   Get out.

Barry   Help him.

Lee   Barry, he's dead – look at me, he's dead.

Barry   Who fuckin did it!

Lee *spots* **Phil** *and* **Becks** *trying to leave.*

Lee   Where you going? You can't leave.

Phil   Oh come on, mate.

Lee   This is a crime scene, no one leaves! Who was last in here?

Lawrie (*feels* **Alan**'s *stare*)   Wat?

Lee   Lawrie?

Lawrie   Oh yeah, here we go.

Lee   You were lass in the toilets.

Lawrie   It weren't me.

Alan   You bloody fool.

Lawrie   Alan, it weren't me, I saw him, thass all.

Barry *runs at* **Lawrie**, *who holds him down, hitting twice in the face.* **Lee** *pulls him off.*

Lee   Lawrie enough, get off him.

Lawrie   I'm gonna line you up next to him.

Lee   Where's the knife, wat you do with it?

Lawrie *spits in his brother's face.*

Lee   Lawrence Bishop. I am arrresting you on suspicion of murder. You do not have to say anything, but it may harm yer defence if you do not mention when questioned something you may rely on in court.

Lawrie *spits in his face again.*

Lee   Anything you do say will be given in evidence. You made me choose.

Jason   This is fucked-up.

Becks   Let us go, Lee.

Lee   No.

Jimmy *comes out, dragging* **Glen** *behind him.*

Gina   Dad?

Jimmy   Gina.

Gina   Wat? Wat!

Jimmy *throws the bloodstained knife onto the bar.*

Gina   No!

Becks   Oh shit.

Lee   Glen, come here.

Gina   No, Glen!

Lee   I said come here.

Barry   It was you!

Lee   Barry, juss back off, yeah.

Barry   Don't you fuckin touch me!

Glen   He's a black bastard, they all are.

Gina   Shut up.

Jimmy   Jesus.

Gina   Hard enuff for you now, Dad?

Jimmy   Gina?

Alan   Rivers of blood.

Barry   You shut yer mout, I'll kill yer. I'll kill all of yer.
Come on, come on! Who wants me, come on! Yer fuckin white
cunts, all of yer! All of yer. Cunts! Come on! Yer white cunts.

Lee   Barry?

Barry   No.

He wipes the paint off his face.

No! No.

Lee *approaches.*

Barry   Fuck off. Get away from me.

Lawrie   Monkey-lover.

Jason (*peers through window*)   Oh shit, they're only coming back.

Phil   Who?

Jason   Fuckin blacks.

Lawrie   No point playin games, Alan.

Alan   I don't know you.

Lawrie   No matter what, it'll come to this.

Sound of police sirens approaching

Lee   Barry?

Barry   No.

Lee (*to* **Barry**)   Don't lose yerself.

Methuen Drama Modern Plays

include work by

Edward Albee
Jean Anouilh
John Arden
Margaretta D'Arcy
Peter Barnes
Sebastian Barry
Brendan Behan
Dermot Bolger
Edward Bond
Bertolt Brecht
Howard Brenton
Anthony Burgess
Simon Burke
Jim Cartwright
Caryl Churchill
Noël Coward
Lucinda Coxon
Sarah Daniels
Nick Darke
Nick Dear
Shelagh Delaney
David Edgar
David Eldridge
Dario Fo
Michael Frayn
John Godber
Paul Godfrey
David Greig
John Guare
Peter Handke
David Harrower
Jonathan Harvey
Iain Heggie
Declan Hughes
Terry Johnson
Sarah Kane
Charlotte Keatley
Barrie Keeffe
Howard Korder

Robert Lepage
Doug Lucie
Martin McDonagh
John McGrath
Terrence McNally
David Mamet
Patrick Marber
Arthur Miller
Mtwa, Ngema & Simon
Tom Murphy
Phyllis Nagy
Peter Nichols
Sean O'Brien
Joseph O'Connor
Joe Orton
Louise Page
Joe Penhall
Luigi Pirandello
Stephen Poliakoff
Franca Rame
Mark Ravenhill
Philip Ridley
Reginald Rose
Willy Russell
Jean-Paul Sartre
Sam Shepard
Wole Soyinka
Shelagh Stephenson
Peter Straughan
C. P. Taylor
Theatre de Complicite
Theatre Workshop
Sue Townsend
Judy Upton
Timberlake Wertenbaker
Roy Williams
Snoo Wilson
Victoria Wood

Methuen Drama Film titles include

The Wings of the Dove
Hossein Armini

Mrs Brown
Jeremy Brock

Persuasion
Nick Dear after Jane Austen

The Gambler
Nick Dear after Dostoyevski

Beautiful Thing
Jonathan Harven

Little Voice
Mark Herman

The Long Good Friday
Barrie Keeffe

State and main
David Mamet

The Crucible
Arthur Miller

The English Patient
Anthony Minghella

The Talented Mr Ripley
Anthony Minghella

Twelfth Night
Trevor Nunn after Shakespeare

The Krays
Philip Ridley

The Reflecting Skin & The Passion of Darkly Noon
Philip Ridley

Trojan Eddie
Billy Roche

Sling Blade
Billy Bob Thornton

The Acid House
Irvine Welsh

Methuen Drama Contemporary Dramatists

include

John Arden (two volumes)
Arden & D'Arcy
Peter Barnes (three volumes)
Sebastian Barry
Dermot Bolger
Edward Bond (six volumes)
Howard Brenton
  (two volumes)
Richard Cameron
Jim Cartwright
Caryl Churchill (two volumes)
Sarah Daniels (two volumes)
Nick Darke
David Edgar (three volumes)
Ben Elton
Dario Fo (two volumes)
Michael Frayn (three volumes)
David Greig
John Godber (two volumes)
Paul Godfrey
John Guare
Lee Hall (two volumes)
Peter Handke
Jonathan Harvey
  (two volumes)
Declan Hughes
Terry Johnson (two volumes)
Sarah Kane
Barrie Keefe
Bernard-Marie Koltès
David Lan
Bryony Lavery
Deborah Levy
Doug Lucie

David Mamet (four volumes)
Martin McDonagh
Duncan McLean
Anthony Minghella
  (two volumes)
Tom Murphy (four volumes)
Phyllis Nagy
Anthony Neilsen
Philip Osment
Louise Page
Stewart Parker (two volumes)
Joe Penhall
Stephen Poliakoff
  (three volumes)
David Rabe
Mark Ravenhill
Christina Reid
Philip Ridley
Willy Russell
Eric-Emmanuel Schmitt
Ntozake Shange
Sam Shepard (two volumes)
Shelagh Stephenson
Wole Soyinka (two volumes)
David Storey (three volumes)
Sue Townsend
Judy Upton
Michel Vinaver
  (two volumes)
Arnold Wesker (two volumes)
Michael Wilcox
Roy Williams
Snoo Wilson (two volumes)
David Wood (two volumes)
Victoria Wood

Methuen Drama World Classics

include

Jean Anouilh (two volumes)
Brendan Behan
Aphra Behn
Bertolt Brecht (eight volumes)
Büchner
Bulgakov
Calderón
Čapek
Anton Chekhov
Noël Coward (eight volumes)
Feydeau
Eduardo De Filippo
Max Frisch
John Galsworthy
Gogol
Gorky (two volumes)
Harley Granville Barker
    (two volumes)
Victor Hugo
Henrik Ibsen (six volumes)
Jarry

Lorca (three volumes)
Marivaux
Mustapha Matura
David Mercer (two volumes)
Arthur Miller (five volumes)
Molière
Musset
Peter Nichols (two volumes)
Joe Orton
A. W. Pinero
Luigi Pirandello
Terence Rattigan
    (two volumes)
W. Somerset Maugham
    (two volumes)
August Strindberg
    (three volumes)
J. M. Synge
Ramón del Valle-Inclán
Frank Wedekind
Oscar Wilde